Talking points

in mathematics

An

CAMBRIDGE
UNIVERSITY PRESS

PUBLISHED BY THE PRESS SYNDICATE OF THE UNIVERSITY OF CAMBRIDGE
The Pitt Building, Trumpington Street, Cambridge, United Kingdom

CAMBRIDGE UNIVERSITY PRESS
The Edinburgh Building, Cambridge CB2 2RU, UK   www.cup.cam.ac.uk
40 West 20th Street, New York, NY 10011-4211, USA   www.cup.org
10 Stamford Road, Oakleigh, Melbourne 3166, Australia
Ruiz de Alarcón 13, 28014 Madrid, Spain

First published 1993
Fifth printing 1999

Printed in the United Kingdom at the University Press, Cambridge

A catalogue record for this book is available from the British Library

ISBN 0 521 44758 5 paperback

Illustrations by Celia Weber

Contents

Introduction   **1**

The purpose of the book   1
Different purposes of language   3
Questioning   6
Working in your head   9
Ways of organising groups   12
Bilingual learners   17
Negotiating meaning   21
Prompting   25
Evaluating discussion   27

Section 1: Rhymes   **31**

Section 2: Talking points described in full   **37**

Number   38
Algebra   51
Shape and space   57
Handling data   69

Section 3: More ideas   **75**

Ordering and place value   76
Measures   83
Doubles and halves   89
Patterns   94
Shapes   101
Position and direction   108
Collecting and presenting data   112
Probability   119

'Then you should say what you mean,' the March Hare
went on.
'I do,' Alice hastily replied; 'at least – I mean what I say –
that's the same thing you know.'

Lewis Carroll: *Alice in Wonderland*

'The time has come,' the Walrus said,
'To talk of many things:
Of shoes – and ships – and sealing wax –
Of cabbages and kings –
Of why the sea is boiling hot –
And whether pigs have wings.'

'When I use a word,' Humpty Dumpty said in a rather
scornful voice, 'it means just what I choose it to mean –
neither more nor less.'
'The question is,' said Alice, 'whether you can make
words mean different things.'

Lewis Carroll: *Through the Looking Glass*

Lewis Carroll was the pen-name of Charles Lutwidge Dodgson,
a lecturer in mathematics at Oxford from 1853 to 1881.

The purpose of the book

The mathematician has many tools of the trade. Pencil and paper are among the most important, and the paper may be plain or coloured, squared or dotty, or even the back of an envelope. Drawing instruments and measuring equipment are essential. So are calculating aids, ranging from conkers and shells to rods and blocks, from the abacus to the electronic calculator. The computer, an even more powerful calculating aid, allows numbers, shapes and other data to be stored, retrieved, manipulated and presented in the form of graphs, diagrams and tables.

There will be a selection of these tools in your classroom. You need to ensure that children become increasingly skilful in selecting the most suitable tool for the task in hand, just as you do in other practical subjects. However, one of a mathematician's most effective tools cannot be seen. It should not be forgotten when the choice of tool is considered!

The Germans have a word for it but there is no direct equivalent in the English language. *Gedankenexperimente*, thought experiments, involve exploring ideas in one's imagination. The exploration might produce a result without further recourse to other mathematical tools, or it may indicate which of the range of tools available would be best to use for the next stage of development. This book of *Talking points* contains suggestions for thought experiments, to encourage children to think and talk about mathematics. The suggestions focus on:

> the use of mathematical vocabulary;
> the use of imagery;
> mental arithmetic strategies.

Mathematical discussion is an activity in its own right as well as a valuable part of other tasks. Its purpose is to clarify and communicate ideas. On many occasions, no apparatus is required, but sometimes the discussion may be supported or stimulated by pictures or objects, and will be followed up by work with other tools, including pencil and paper.

Sadly, children are frequently expected to write mathematics before they have learned to imagine and to discuss, and those who do not easily make connections are offered more pencil and paper work instead of the vital talk and discussion. Yet in other subjects it would be unthinkable to ask children to write what they cannot say.

The introductory section of the book explains how work might be planned and organised. It is not intended to be read in any particular order and you can start with whichever part seems to capture your interest.

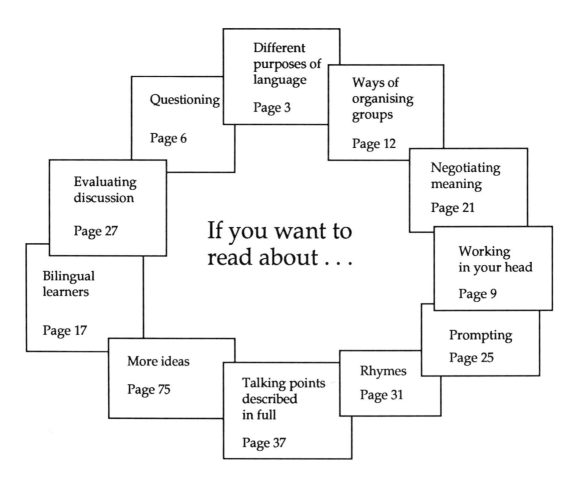

The rest of the book provides different ideas to support five or more minutes of talking about mathematics, arranged in three sections: number rhymes, talking points described in full, and lots more ideas described briefly.

Different purposes of language

Children who have wide experience of using language for different purposes are more likely to feel confident about expressing themselves. The different types of talk which children might encounter were identified in the National Oracy Project: telling, narrating, reporting, informing, summarising, explaining, questioning or responding to questions, exploring, suggesting, hypothesising, speculating, arguing, persuading, collaborating, imagining, expressing feelings, evaluating.

The programmes of study for speaking and listening in the National Curriculum prescribe the activities that should be available across the curriculum. There is some overlap between the activities for each key stage; the main difference between them is in their degree of complexity or level of detail. Some of the activities, with examples that could be used in mathematics, are given for you below.

Listening to or telling stories, poems and songs, including examples from different cultures and from pupils' own work

Who can say the rhyme about five little ducks?
On the table there are six 1p and one 10p coin. Can you make up a story in which they are used?
Do you know about the Emperor Fuh-hi, the turtle and the magic square?
This graph tells a story. What might the story be?

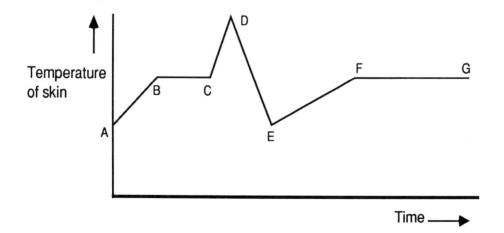

Asking and responding to questions

Which of these shapes would roll in a straight line?
If the answer is 16, what is the question?
What can you tell me about angles?

Giving or responding to explanations, information or instructions

What instructions would make the floor turtle go round the chair?
What time is it? How long is it until lunch time?
What tiling patterns are there around the school?
Why is the sum of two odd numbers always even?
Explain why each angle of an equilateral triangle is 60°.

Describing experiences or recounting events

Tell us how you spent your time on Saturday.
What happened when you pressed 2 + = = = = on your calculator? What else did you try?
Shut your eyes and imagine two circles. Now slide one of the circles towards the other. What did you see?

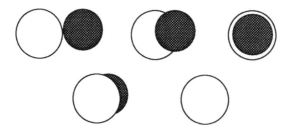

Expressing opinions, and justifying them

Look at these pieces of fabric. Which is your favourite pattern?
What shape is in the feely-bag? Why do you think it's a ...?
Do people with blue eyes usually have fair hair?
Do people with longer legs run faster? How could we find out?

Planning collaboratively

How would you put these parcels in order of their weight?
Plan how to investigate which numbers divide exactly by 6.
If you had £1 million to spend, how would you spend it?
Using the timetables and maps, plan a route to Paris.

Presenting and explaining information or ideas logically

My five coins total 75p. What might they be? Why?
Describe to us how you might make an envelope.
Can you explain your strategy for Noughts and Crosses?

1 First you do your cross on any
fo The corners. 2 Then the next
Per Son gos 3. You Put another cross
on another corner 4. Next Person gos
5 Then you Put The cross on another
corner so You>ve got Two holes
between the Cross 6
Next Peson goes ┌ cross can go how
and win

Predicting, speculating and hypothesising

Guess which of these containers will hold the most water.
Is it likely to rain tomorrow? What reasons do you have?
How many children will there be in the school in three years' time?

Reporting and summarising

What different shapes did you make with your four squares?
What did you discover about the growth of your bean?
Tell us about your survey, how you set about it and what you found out.
Do you think that your game of Snakes and Ladders was fair?

Questioning

One of the purposes of language is to ask and respond to questions.

There are many different types of questions in mathematics, ranging from those that are answered by simple recall of facts to those that involve problem solving skills. Try to use a balance between the different types and to use open questions. A closed question like *What are four threes?* has a single right answer. Open questions like *If the answer is 12, what is the question?* or *If you know that $7 \times 6 = 42$, what else can you work out?* have many possible responses, and allow children to suggest ideas according to their ability.

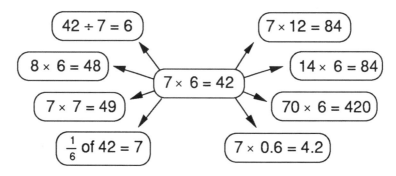

Different types of questions

Listed below are some examples of different types of questions. There is a tendency for the first two categories, which involve recalling and applying facts, to be used far more often than the last four categories, each of which requires a higher level of thinking. Try to use all types of questions over a period and to encourage children to give more than short answers.

Recalling facts
What are three fours?
How many centimetres are there in a metre?
What is this shape called?

Applying facts
Is this triangle equilateral?
What is the width of the table to the nearest centimetre?
What are the factors of 42?

Hypothesising or predicting
Can you estimate the number of marbles in this jar?
Is there a connection between eye colour and hair colour?
How many rectangles in the next diagram? And the next?

Designing procedures
How might we count this pile of sticks?
How could we test a number to see if it is divisible by 6?
How could we find the 20th triangular number?
Are there other ways of doing it?

Interpreting results
So what does that tell us about numbers that end in five or zero?
What does the graph tell us about the most common shoe size?
So what can we say about the sum of the angles in a triangle?

Applying reasoning
The seven coins in my purse total 23p. What could they be?
How many different ways can four children sit at a round table?
Why is the sum of two consecutive triangular numbers always square?

Children's own questions

You should also encourage children to ask questions, not simply respond to those that you ask. Getting them to suggest questions is easier if you have some objects, a picture or a pattern as a starting point: for example,

two leaves
three dice
three different coins
five straws of different sizes
two identical boxes, one filled with small pebbles, one with marbles
a set of containers

To take one of these examples, with five straws of different lengths, a range of questions can be asked, depending on the age and attainment of the children.

How many straws? Which is the longest? Estimate the length of each one.
Make some shapes with the straws. Now describe the shapes.
Can you make a five pointed star?
What is the maximum number of triangles you can make?
What is the biggest area you can enclose?
Can you arrange the straws to intersect in ten different places?

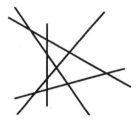

At first, when children suggest questions that can be asked, these are likely to be those that start with phrases like:

How many ...?
How much ...?
How long is ...?
What is the most/least ...?

With encouragement, they will be able to suggest questions that begin:

Can we describe ...?
What is the same/different about ...?
How could we make a ...?
How could we find out ...?
Can we estimate or predict ...?
How many different ways are there of ...?

To broaden the scope of their questions, you might then suggest that they try to ask questions that start with these phrases:

Can we explain ...?
Why is ...?
What would happen if ...?

Working in your head

The advantage of thinking aloud is that it allows ideas to be shared as they develop. But not all thinking needs to be aloud; some may be done silently. The thinking involved could be working out a mental calculation, reflecting on the method used, considering a way of solving a problem, visualising a shape, pattern, arrangement or diagram, animating an imaginary figure ...

Mental arithmetic

Every adult needs to be able to calculate mentally. The handling of money, giving change by the shopkeeper's method of counting on, reckoning of journey times and calculations involving measurements of various kinds are all carried out mentally in daily life. Even the pencil and paper methods of calculating are based on steps which are done in the head. The 'tens and units' addition of $25 + 67$ requires the mental calculations $5 + 7 = 12$ and $1 + 2 + 6 = 9$; the division of 594 by 27 involves mental experiment with multiples of 27. Skill in mental methods of calculation therefore helps the understanding and development of written methods.

However, few people use the standard written methods when they are working in their heads. For example, it is common when calculating mentally to add the hundreds or the tens first and then the units, or the pounds before the pence. You need to point this out to the children and discuss the variety of methods which it is acceptable to use. There is no 'proper' method – children should choose whatever method suits them best.

Good mental methods are based on the understanding of place value together with recall of addition and multiplication facts. You need to build up children's speed and confidence in the recall of number facts, and to extend their awareness of the number system, without worrying about formal recording.

There are various strategies you can use to ensure that each child responds during a session requiring mental arithmetic. With younger children, you can give each member of the group a set of cards, double width for numerals 10 to 90, and single width for numerals 1 to 9.

| **4 0** | with | **6** | gives | **4 6** |

When you ask a question, each child places the appropriate units card on top of the tens card, and holds it still on the table top while you check their responses. Older pupils can, of course, write their answers. An alternative is to provide them with counters and a mixed set of Bingo boards. As questions are asked, numbers corresponding to answers can be covered on the boards.

12	41	86	94
23	18	27	10
9	32	21	7
15	66	52	40

Reflecting on methods

It is important that you plan times when you describe to children the thought processes through which you reached a result, so that they learn from your strategies. Similarly, they can learn from each other. Threaded through all the talking points you develop with them should be requests for them to explain their thinking and methods to you and their peers. This might include their descriptions of the thinking that led nowhere, the reason why a different path was pursued or why one thing was done rather than another.

Imagery

There is a danger that mathematics is seen by children as a subject in which they learn about other people's ideas, particularly yours, and that it has little to do with them. Use of imagery helps children to appreciate that mathematics can be personal – something which they can create for themselves – and that there can be different ways of seeing and thinking about a mathematical idea.

Imagery includes all aspects of thinking or mental activity which help to make sense of a particular idea. It can draw on all five senses – sight, hearing, touch, taste and smell – but in mathematics the last two will play only a very tiny part. The strongest will be the first – the ability to picture or to visualise numbers, shapes or other objects, and to manipulate them.

Working in your head

For many of us, the things that we remember and recapture most vividly are those for which we have clear images. Most adults will have experienced a sound or smell which takes them back to a previous event as if it were only yesterday. If children are to recapture mathematical ideas just as clearly then they need vivid and enjoyable experiences which they will be able to recall. They can then reconstruct for themselves things that are important. For many children, experiences which start *I want you to imagine ...* are among the most engrossing that take place in school and usually lead to animated discussion in which everyone is keen to tell what they have 'seen'.

Let's take an example.

Imagine a white circle. Put a small spot of black paint on it. Where is the spot? At the centre? On the circumference? Or is it somewhere in between? Move the spot to the edge of the circle. Now turn the circle slowly about its centre so that the spot of paint leaves a trace. What happens? Stop the circle so that the spot of paint is at the bottom of the circle. Now, in your imagination, set the circle rolling along a straight line. What trace does the black spot leave now?

Did you actually 'see' what was happening?

One child's mental image of something may be very different from another child's, yet each can be valued and shared. Activities in which children can develop their own images of a mathematical idea allows each of them to start with their own perception and to move together to a common understanding.

<table>
<tr><td>

Imagine you are flying
above your house.

What will you see?
How will things look?

</td><td>

Hannah

</td></tr>
</table>

in the magic garden I bit a
magic apple and I could fly
and my mummy was loking
for me and I could see
all around the world and
the people were tiny

11

Ways of organising groups

The best way of organising the class will depend on the type of discussion you want to arrange. You may want all the children to gather round you as a whole class or you may prefer to work with a smaller number. On the other hand, you may want a group of children to hold the discussion on their own and to join them every so often.

Talking with the whole class

Talking with a whole class is usually for question and answer sessions. Younger children usually sit on a carpeted area of floor; older pupils might need to move some of the classroom furniture so that a group atmosphere is created. Alternatively, you could use an open area such as a television room, the library or the hall, if these are not in use. Children should sit so that each of them can see the focal point of the discussion, whether this is you, a picture, some apparatus or the blackboard. Try to involve as many children as possible and look out for any whose interest is flagging.

You need to take care not to dominate what is happening, whatever the size of the group. There is research evidence to suggest that on average a teacher talks for three-quarters of the time in the class situation; in 20 minutes, this gives each child about 10 seconds to speak!

You can build in a waiting time before asking for responses, to encourage a greater number of children to offer a suggestion, especially after *Why ...?* and *How ...?* questions, but it is sometimes more appropriate for children to talk in pairs or threes for a short period. This encourages all children to respond by sharing with a partner before public answers are accepted and helps to avoid situations where the most articulate dominate much of the dialogue. Another strategy is to divide the class into groups and ask questions of each in turn, or to ask girls and boys in turn in order to maintain a gender balance.

Joining a smaller group for talk

Small group work, on the other hand, can provide a security that encourages the less articulate to play a greater part in the exchange. If you are trying this out for the first time, it is helpful if there is another adult to support the other children in the class while you work with the group. A group of four to six children works best. The adult providing support could be the headteacher or the mathematics coordinator, but it could also be a parent or a classroom assistant. Either way, helpers need to be briefed carefully about the work you have planned for the rest of the class and the role you would like them to play.

In a session of one hour with classroom support you could spend 10 minutes or so with each of five groups. You need to allow time for someone helping you to tell you how other children worked and what they might next need to do.

More commonly, you will be working on your own with all the children. Ten minutes with a different group on each day of the week is easier to manage and is less trying on the patience of the rest of the class. They need to be settled at tasks that they can pursue without interrupting you, as far as possible. Make sure that they know that they should not bother you except in a crisis!

A well organised classroom in which children can select what they need for themselves is half the secret. Have good supplies of different kinds of paper readily available, and pencils and pens in varied colours. Suitable calculators and dictionaries should be on hand. Have other activities available for children to carry on with if they finish a piece of work and you are still talking with a group: for example, a box of mathematical games and puzzles, or suggestions written on cards.

If you have finished

Investigate
How can three children
divide £3 between them?

£3

```
1₮      1₮      1₮

1 50    1₮   50p
2₮      50p  50p
1 50P   140P  10P
90P     10P   2₮
80P     20P 2₮
70P     30P  2₮
```

Plan the discussion carefully and think of three or four ways in which it might develop, using notes if necessary. Make sure children sit facing each other and make yourself part of the group. It is important that everyone can see each other so that no one feels left out.

A real discussion can only be sustained if children have enough confidence and are sure that their contributions will be valued. A receptive silence is often as important as speaking in encouraging them to talk. If they are reluctant at first, get them to go over in their minds what has just been said or to explain their thinking to others in the group. Encourage them to ask questions of other children: *Who would like to ask Sarah a question about her idea?* If possible, try to avoid telling children that they are wrong. Ask: *What do other people think?* or *How could we check that?* Praise their contributions wherever possible.

A group of children talking on their own

When you want children to talk on their own, you might first set the scene with the whole class, describing the talking point and posing questions for children to think about. Small groups can then be set to talk, each pursuing its own train of thought. You can spend a little time with each group, encouraging the children either to develop or to clarify points in their thinking, or taking them beyond their initial thoughts to other possibilities. An alternative is to spend more time with just one or two groups, varying the groups on each occasion.

Where children talk together in a group, membership may need to change from time to time so that they gain experience of working with different people. Sometimes groups will be of the same ability, sometimes of mixed ability. Friends usually work together well. You will need to be alert to dominating behaviour, and you may, on occasions, decide to form single sex groups. For some discussions either you or the group may want to assign roles to particular members: for example, leading the discussion, taking notes, drawing diagrams, leading the presentation, and so on. Children who are very able and who are quick to suggest ideas may need to be asked to manage the discussion in order to allow others to contribute.

Have ready an extension activity to give to any group that reaches a conclusion quickly. This will allow those that take longer enough time to fine-tune their thinking.

Consecutive sums

Now try the numbers
from 20 to 30.

$20 = 2+3+4+5+6$

$21 = 10 + 11$

$22 = 7+6+5+4$

$23 = 11 + 12$

$24 = 7 + 8 + 9$

$25 = 13 + 12$

$26 = 8+7+6+5$

$27 = 8+9+10$

$28 = 1+2+3+4+5+6+7$

$29 = 15+14$

$30 = 4+5+6+7+8$

Presenting conclusions to others

All discussion can be followed up by pencil and paper or other activities, if this is appropriate, but try to arrange things so that small group talk is followed by sharing with at least one other group or even with the whole class. Your role here is not only to listen and to praise, but also to make sure that each group gives a full explanation of its thinking and justifies its decisions.

You will need to teach children how best to organise their presentations to their peers. The exploratory dialogue that takes place in a small group will not serve when ideas are presented to the whole class. For one thing, there is less security about the situation, since what can be chanced in a small group may be less acceptable if presented to all the children. The presentation needs to have a sense of direction, in which thoughts follow one from the other in a logical way. The group must choose its presenters, who should not always be the same, more articulate children. The presenters should take into account the variety of listeners and aim to hold their attention. Ideas should be carefully explained so that other children can follow them. Members of the group must be prepared to elaborate if they are questioned by you or by other children.

A presentation can take many forms. It may be visual, perhaps a wall display like that on page 16, or a pattern, model or construction placed on a table; it may be written, possibly accompanied by diagrams, tables or charts; it may be oral, perhaps a planned dialogue with different members of the group making different points and afterwards summarising their conclusions. You might decide to make notes on a blackboard or wall chart so that ideas from presentations can be compared. At the end of a sharing session you can pull together any ideas that the groups hold in common and identify any major differences.

A display of some arrangements of four ...

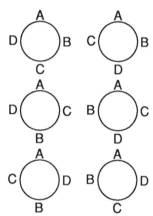

Right-angled isosceles triangles

People at a round table

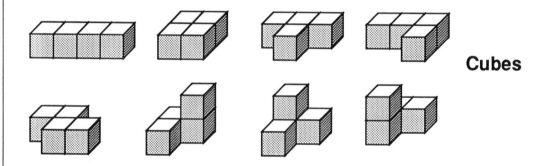

Cubes

Circles: no intersections

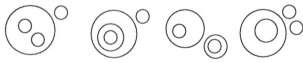

4321	4312	4231	4213	4132	4123
3421	3412	3241	3214	3142	3124
2431	2413	2341	2314	2143	2134
1432	1423	1342	1324	1243	1234

Digits

Bilingual learners

In lots of classes there are bilingual children from homes where a language other than English is usually spoken. Some bilingual children speak English fluently; others may speak just a few words. If you have pupils in your class whose command of the English language is limited, your role has a dual challenge: to help them with the early stages of speaking and listening to English as a 'foreign' language, while at the same time challenging their mathematical thinking at the highest level of which they are capable.

It is important that these two issues are not confused; it is very easy to assume that because the language needs to be simple, so does the mathematical activity. Children who have already learned to measure to a suitable degree of accuracy do not need to repeat that learning, but they do need help in acquiring familiarity with the names and sizes of the commonly used metric and imperial units of measurement.

How best to support children who are not yet fluent in English may depend on the skills of other pupils in the class. A large group of children speaking the same home language can support each other on occasions, but may be less likely to practise their spoken English. The best climate for supporting the language development of a class with dual language skills can be based on the following strategies.

The classroom environment

Label your mathematics area, equipment and materials in both languages and point to the labels when you refer to the equipment. For younger children, provide bilingual number games, tapes of number songs and rhymes in the home language, and so on. Provide audio-tapes in slowly spoken English to help children with rules of games, and keyboard overlays to help with input to computer programs. You can also set up wall displays of commonly used words and phrases. Make sure that there is a number line displayed with numerals in both scripts.

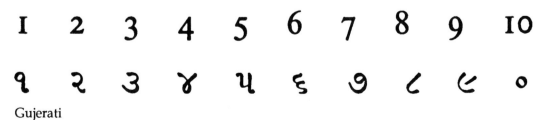

Gujerati

Mathematical activities

Some of all children's mathematical activities can be based on things with which the bilingual children in the class are particularly familiar: for example, stories, everyday activities, festivals, objects brought from home, food and drinks, customary styles of dress, familiar people and places. Use pictures, photographs and diagrams to accompany any explanations. Make sure that plenty of practical apparatus and other visual aids are available throughout.

Most games of strategy, whatever their country of origin, whether in the form of a computer program or a board game, can be demonstrated and played with relatively little spoken language. After the game, a discussion about good moves and what worked well helps all children to crystallise what was important about the activity. It also provides an opportunity for practising skills of summarising.

Lau Kati Kata

This game is from Bengal.
Each player has six pieces.
Moves are along a line to an adjacent point.
Pieces are captured by being jumped over.
More than one capture can be made in a move.
What is the quickest possible game?

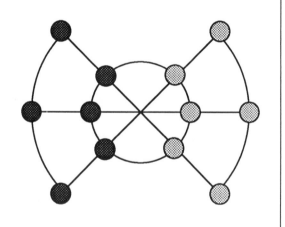

Use of language

When you are talking to bilingual children, plan carefully what you are going to say to make sure that your meaning is conveyed effectively. It is not necessary for every single word to be understood. Keep your vocabulary simple at first and extend gradually the range you use.

You can reinforce what you say in a number of ways: for example,

- through gesture, mime and your facial expression;
- by using visual clues, such as signs and symbols, pictures and flash cards, or diagrams and maps;
- by slowing down speech in key places;
- by giving extra emphasis to important words;
- through interspersing the familiar with the unfamiliar.

Use plenty of repetition of important terms and use practical apparatus or classroom objects to help you demonstrate. You might encourage all children in the class to make their own illustrated mathematical dictionary and add to it as they learn new words. Watch out and listen for positive responses and praise any success, however small.

Grouping

If possible, pair children who speak the same home language so that one child who is more fluent in English can help another who is less so. Integrate pairs of bilingual pupils with groups of native English speakers at the same level of mathematical ability, and challenge the latter to make their instructions, comments and explanations really clear. Make sure that bilingual learners know and can use confidently phrases like *I don't understand* or *What does that mean?* or *Say that again* in order to ask other children for help. Teach them early on to use phrases like *Your turn* or *I've won* when playing a game.

Recording work

Allow bilingual pupils plenty of time to observe and listen; they need not be expected to talk or write in English before they are ready. Children can show their understanding through non-verbal responses such as carrying out instructions to draw, make, build, continue a pattern, arrange, move, reflect, turn, count, calculate, measure, plot ...

Bilingual pupils who have learned to write in their home or first language soon acquire the skill of writing the international set of numerals: 1, 2, 3, 4, 5 and so on. Nevertheless, it is important that they are asked to do more than 'sums'.

Give them plenty of opportunities to present their mathematical work as a picture or pattern, diagram or graph, or three-dimensional model. When you are making an assessment of what they have achieved, or when they are explaining their ideas to you, make sure that any practical apparatus that they might need to help them is available.

Classroom support

Invite any staff whose job it is to help bilingual pupils to give you any insights they have on the development of the mathematics curriculum: for example, where the order of work might be altered, where it is too wordy and how it might be made more visual. Ask them also to take part in some mathematical activities. Try to liaise closely with any community language teachers and bilingual parents and ask them if possible to focus attention on the significant mathematical vocabulary that you are using with the class.

Monitoring progress

Here are some examples of the possible developments in all pupils' use of language in mathematics.

At first	Later on
Responding with one word or a short phrase	Making longer statements
Using informal vocabulary	Using correct mathematical vocabulary
Asking a simple or short question	Asking more complex questions
Asking for help	Providing help
Making a brief comment	Giving reasons or explanations
Using standard phrases	Suggesting questions or activities
Giving a simple opinion	Justifying a point of view
Making a simple choice	Negotiating and persuading others

Negotiating meaning

Full understanding of the words and ideas associated with mathematics develops over time. There are several strategies to draw on that can help children to grasp meaning and to use confidently an increasingly precise mathematical vocabulary.

Using everyday language

For many children, the first step in solving a problem is to try to put it into ordinary everyday language to clarify what it means. You will often have asked children in your class to say in their own words what they think they have been asked to do or what they have done so far. Very often, the process of talking will clarify what is needed next.

Using a variety of descriptions of relationships

Through describing relationships in different ways, some informal and some formal, you can help children to understand the connections between mathematical ideas. To take a simple example, think of some of the different ways you can ask about the relationship between 2, 3 and 5.

> What is 2 and 3?
> What is 2 add on 3?
> 2 plus 3 equals ...?
> What is the sum of/total of 2 and 3?
> If you count on 3 from 2, you get to ...?
> What is 3 more than 2?
> What should we add to 2 to make 5?
> What is 5 take away 3?
> 5 minus 3 equals ...?
> If we subtract 3 from 5, we get ...?
> What is the difference between 5 and 3?
> If you count back 3 from 5, you get to ...?
> How many more than 3 is 5?
> How many fewer than 5 is 3?
> When I take 3 from a number, I get 2. What is the number?
> What did I start with if, when I added 3, I got 5?

If you wish, you can give these questions a context by starting by saying: *I want you to think of a number line* or *Imagine you have a small pile of counters*. Other contexts can be provided by relating the statements to objects like sweets, to measures like cups of milk or to the use of money.

Extending vocabulary

Another aim is to extend gradually the informal vocabulary used by young children to a more formal mathematical vocabulary. Early meanings that are associated with a word like 'round', for example, need to be refined to give a more precise description through the use of adjectives like concave, convex, circular, spherical, cylindrical, and nouns like circle, circumference, arc, spiral, sphere, ellipse, cylinder, cone, torus, annulus, and so on. It is not uncommon to find pupils in the early years of secondary schooling looking blank when faced with words like 'product' or 'divide' simply because they are still using the informal 'times' or 'share'.

In negotiating meanings of new vocabulary with children, the starting point needs to be their own natural language and the end point the formal language of mathematics. Each child needs to trace the steps from the familiar to the new, from the idea which she or he already has to that which is to be acquired. To achieve this, you need to build upon the children's contributions, which indicate where their thinking now stands, and move sensitively towards the vocabulary that is technically correct.

To introduce as an intermediary stage your own informal language may seem useful at times, but needs to be treated with care. For example, if teachers help children to remember that the horizontal coordinate comes before the vertical by using phrases like 'walk before you climb', this phrase may not be known to the next teacher and so may later cause confusion.

One way of helping children to appreciate the precision of the mathematical vocabulary associated with shape and space is to have a selection of cards with diagrams or patterns on them. Children then pick a card from the pack and, without showing you, they describe what they see on the card. You then draw for them exactly what they have described, being careful to do no more than that.

For example, the children might pick a card showing this.

The dialogue that follows might then go something like this.

The children might say:	You draw and say:

We can see two hexagons.

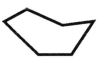

I've drawn two hexagons.

The sides are the same length.

All the sides are the same length.

The angles are the same.

They're both regular hexagons.

They're the same size.

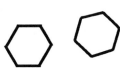

Turn the right one round so the top edges point in the same direction.

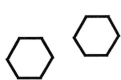

They have the same orientation. The top edges are parallel.

They're level with
each other.

They're at the same horizontal
level.

They touch at a corner.

They touch at a vertex.

Meanings in mathematics

You may also need to help children distinguish between the meaning of a word in mathematics and its meaning in everyday use. Just think, for example, of the different meanings of these words.

angle	even	prime
average	face	product
base	factor	quarters
bearing	foot	root
cancel	mass	row
chord	match	scale
closed	mean	score
correspondence	multiply	table
cycle	odd	times
diamond	power	volume

Every classroom needs a mathematical dictionary which children can refer to. Mathematical dictionaries suitable for primary aged children are available from educational publishers, but children generally enjoy creating their own class dictionary, with illustrations and carefully worded mathematical definitions.

Prompting

However carefully you organise talking activities, there will be times when exchange of ideas flows less readily. Your role is to prompt the children's thinking, rather than to give them specific information about what to do. Listed below are some examples of the kinds of prompts that are useful in particular circumstances.

Clarifying a problem

In the early stages of working out what is required, you might ask:

- What are you asked to do?
- What question are you trying to answer?
- What information do you have?
- What is the best way to organise the information?
- Can you get any more information?
- Would it help to think of a diagram?

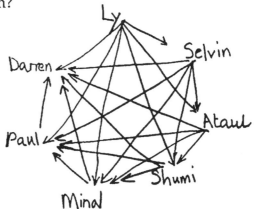

> Some children shook hands with each other.
>
> Investigate the number of handshakes.

Getting going

When children are working out how to attack a problem, you might ask:

- What did you do last time?
- So what is different this time?
- Could you try a particular case? For example, what happens when seven children shake hands?
- What would happen with a simpler problem – three children rather than seven, four numbers instead of five, a square instead of a rectangle ...?
- Why not make a guess and see what happens?
- Would it help to work backwards?
- What can you eliminate – what won't work?

Stepping stones

When a problem has been partly solved, you might ask:

- What have you done so far? What do you still need to do?
- Is there any information you haven't used yet?
- Would it help to put things in order?
- Would a graph help? Or a diagram?
- How many possibilities have you got?
- Is there a pattern? How could you use it?

Ly shook 6 peoples hands
Selvin shook 5 peoples hands
Ataul shook 4 peoples hands
shumi shook 3 peoples hands
minal shook 2 peoples hands
paul shook 1 person's hand.
Darren shook 0 person's hands

What equaled 21 hand shakes

And if, in spite of prompts, children find the problem too hard to solve, they should feel able to put it away until tomorrow, next week or even next year, without feeling inadequate. Real mathematicians rarely solve problems at their first attempt, and almost never in the neat time slot between break and lunch!

Extensions

On the other hand, a group that quickly reaches a conclusion can be encouraged to broaden the scope of the discussion. You might suggest:

- How can you be sure that you have thought of all the possibilities?
- What if you changed the numbers, changed the shape, changed the rules ...?
- What if you started with a rectangle rather than a square?
- What if you could only use ...?
- What if there were more of them?

Evaluating discussion

You will want to make careful assessments of children's progress and consider the implications for your work. In thinking about approaches to mathematical talk, both in your classroom and more generally within the school, there are certain questions that you can ask. The answers will help to highlight what might need to be done.

General questions about provision in your school

- Do school guidelines identify how often, and for what purposes, talk with the whole class and talk with small groups should take place?

- How are children's experiences of mathematical talk made progressively more challenging? Has it been possible to compare the work done by two age groups who have used the same talking point?

- How do teachers in your school know what talking points children have previously engaged in?

- Are any classroom helpers given guidance about what to do? Are parents encouraged to assist? Is there a booklet to tell parents how they might capitalise on situations at home? For example:

LEARNING FROM DOMESTIC TASKS

Most day-to-day activities in a home involve some mathematical experiences and talking about them casually will bring these out. Chores like cooking, washing up, tidying away and going shopping will involve measuring, sorting, comparing capacities of containers, estimating and calculating.

LEARNING FROM TOYS AND GAMES

Construction kits provide opportunities to discuss shapes and their position. Most board games and card games help to develop ideas of counting moves, working out strategies and keeping scores.

LEARNING ON WALKS

The outdoor environment offers many possibilities for observing and talking about mathematics. The patterns of numbers on doors, bricks in a wall or tiles on a footpath can all be discussed. Look for shapes such as squares, triangles and circles in road signs, windows or doors. The fronts of houses and arrangements of gardens are often symmetrical. Spot numbers on cars, doors, shop fronts, buses . . .

Evaluating discussion

Questions to ask yourself about your role

- Do you allow sufficient time for talking points?

- Would children in your class see you as someone who is enthusiastic about mathematical discussion?

- Do you:
  prepare thoroughly when you are planning sessions of talk;
  spend enough time listening to and observing children rather than talking yourself;
  remember not to intervene when children are trying to sort things out for themselves;
  allow enough time for each group of children to mull things over;
  spend sufficient time getting children to explain their thinking and methods to you and to other children;
  follow up talking points when it is appropriate to do so?

NOTES ON GROUP DISCUSSION	By you	By the children
Asking questions		
Answering questions		
Reflecting, imagining		
Calculating mentally		
Describing methods or thinking		

- Could you improve the integration of talking points with other activities?

- Do you cater adequately for each individual child? Have you checked that each child gets an equal amount of time to talk, and that particular children do not dominate within a group? Do you have good strategies for helping those children whose home language is other than English to take part?

- Do you keep sufficiently good notes of the progress each child is making?

Assessing children's achievements

Assessing what children have achieved in a session of talk is never easy. It not only involves listening carefully to what they say; it also involves observing them and considering their attitudes towards each other and towards the topic being discussed. You need to watch how children approach their discussion, whether they enjoy it and whether it challenges them. As part of your assessment you need to ask children to justify their remarks, to explain their methods and to give reasons for their results.

When you are reflecting on a particular discussion, you will need to think about the role that you played, the general flow of the conversation and the main statements made by the children. There may have been moments when a 'breakthrough' occurred and one or more members of the group gained an insight into something of significance.

Some questions to think about are these.

- How readily did the group understand the talking point?

- Did all the children enjoy taking part? How did their enjoyment compare with their enjoyment of other aspects of classroom work?

- What problems did they have and how did they overcome them?

- Were both boys and girls equally confident and equally articulate?

- Did one child always take the lead? Did each child listen carefully and respect the contributions of others? How cooperative were they?

- What vocabulary did they use confidently? Did any child use a new word for the first time?

- Did the group help each other to interpret information in order to make sense of and absorb the details?

- Did they use logical connectives to reason with each other: if, then, because, otherwise, and, either, or ...?

- Did they consider in advance the possible outcomes of their decisions, and predict the results that they expected to obtain?

- Did their conversation reveal that they were looking for relationships: for example, did they use phrases like *that's the same as ..., that's less than before, it should go in front of ..., they seem to be going up together ...?*

- When questioned, could they explain and justify their strategies? Could they describe and give possible reasons for their results?

- When you reflect upon a particular discussion, can you identify moments when a particular child was: defining; describing; hypothesising; predicting; explaining; reasoning; justifying?

- Did any child reveal new knowledge or understanding, either in the initial discussion or in the follow-up work? If so, how can this be built upon?

- Did any follow-up work reflect the quality and totality of what was said in the discussion? If not, does this matter?

- What would be gained by encouraging children to extend their recorded work into a more complete description of their methods, strategies and conclusions?

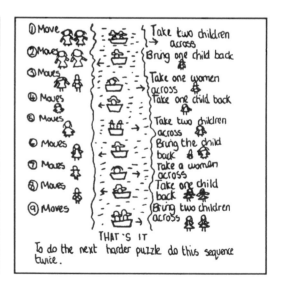

Rhymes

There are three sections setting out examples of talking points for you to try. This first section is short and is devoted to rhymes. Rhymes, like good stories, can be told and retold until they become totally familiar. Saying rhymes in unison with other children can generate confidence in those who are more reluctant to speak; they are then more likely to respond in any follow-up discussion. The rhyme can provide a context for new terminology and help to make its meaning more explicit. Humour in a rhyme is often a motivating factor and the rhythm can help children to commit counting sequences to memory.

Children generally enjoy making a class book of all the mathematical rhymes that they know. The rhymes can be illustrated or the words changed to create new, slightly different rhymes. In these ways they become 'owned' by those who say them.

Most of the rhymes in this section are suitable for the 4 to 9 age group, linked to these levels of the curriculum.

Counting	Number	Level 1
Addition and subtraction	Number	Levels 2, 3
Counting in groups	Number	Level 3
Multiplication and division	Number	Levels 3, 4 or 5
Shapes	Shape and space	Levels 1, 2 or 3

Two of the multiplication and division rhymes are puzzles to stretch children who are more able. In one of these puzzles, in particular, a calculator might be necessary.

Counting

The letter box is round and red.
Its hole is very wide.
I'm going to post twelve letters
And drop them down inside.

One, two, three …

Vary the number of letters posted.

I have a little chiming clock,
I love to hear it ring.
Every day at one o'clock
It … goes … TING!

I have a little chiming clock,
I love to hear it ring.
Every day at two o'clock
It … goes … TING! TING!

Go on from here.
You can clap to the chimes.

Five big balloons,
I'm holding in my hand.
All of a sudden,
One goes BANG!

Four big balloons …

Go on from here.
An alternative is to start with ten
balloons and for two to pop each time.

How many paces will I take
To walk across the floor?
Count the paces for me
As I walk up to the door.

One, two, three …

Nine blue skittles in a row.
Knock them over as you go.

Nine, eight, seven …

Vary the number and colour.

A tall silver rocket
Is standing on the ground.
Now it's nearly ready.
Here comes the sound.

Ten, nine, eight …

BLAST OFF!

Addition and subtraction

Two children having lots of fun
Are swinging on the gate.
How many more must come along
To make them up to eight?

Start with a different small number.

I've twelve meat pies to sell today.
Pay me a pound and take two away.

I've ten meat pies to sell today.
Pay me a pound and take two away.

Go on from here.
How much was I paid?

Open the oven.
It's very hot.
Put in the loaves.
In they pop.
Four inside
And six on top.

How many loaves altogether?
Vary the numbers inside and on top.

My twenty coloured handkerchiefs
Are hanging on the line.
How many of them must I take
In order to leave nine?

Vary the starting number each time.

A fat green crocodile
Eats men alive.
He's eaten one already –
Four more will make it five.

A fat green crocodile
Eats men alive.
He's eaten two already –
Three more will make it five.

Go on from here.

Cluckety, cluck! Cluckety, cluck!
Here's my hen.
How many chicks
Does she have today?
She has ten.
Three are yellow.
Four are brown.
Some are speckled
And covered in down.

How many chicks are speckled?
Change the numbers of yellow and
brown chicks each time.

Counting in groups

Twenty red skittles,
All in a pile.
Stand the skittles in a row,
For a little while.

Two, four, six . . .

Twenty red skittles,
Standing in a row.
Knock the skittles down again
As you go.

Twenty, eighteen, sixteen …

*Vary the number of skittles and choose
how many to move each time.*

Ch'ing T'ou Leng, fly the kite.
Len'g T'ou Ch'ing, spin the top.
Seng Seng Tien, beat the drum.
Tien Seng Seng, bang the gong.
Peng Hu Lu Pa, ring the bell.
Pa Lu Hu Peng, count in tens.

Ten, twenty, thirty, forty, fifty, sixty.

This is a Chinese rhyme from Beijing.

Two and two are four,
Four and four are eight,
Eight and eight are sixteen,
Sixteen and sixteen are thirty-two.

*This can be sung as a round to the tune
from The King and I.*

Ten hopping frogs,
Sitting on a well,
Two jumped in,
And down they fell.

Eight hopping frogs,
Sitting on a well,
Two jumped in,
And down they fell.

*Go on from here.
The starting number can be varied,
as can the number which fall in.*

Two, four, six, eight.
Meet me at the garden gate.
If I'm late, don't wait.
Two, four, six, eight.

Traditional American rhyme.

Fifteen little apples,
Hanging from a tree.
Shake the little apples,
And down come three.

Twelve little apples,
Hanging from a tree.
Shake the little apples,
And down come three.

*Go on from here.
Vary the starting number. It does
not need to be a multiple of three.*

Multiplication and division

Five big lions
And twenty pounds of meat.
How many pounds
Does each lion eat?

*Vary the number of lions and the
number of pounds of meat.*

Three-leaved clover
Growing in a ring.
Three leaves together
Count them as we sing.

Three, six, nine …

*How many clover did you count?
Repeat with four-leaved clover.*

Nine times this and five times that
Add up to sixty-two.
If you can tell me what this is
That's all you have to do.

For more able pupils with a calculator.

Start off with me. Divide by seven,
Then just for fun add on eleven;
Now multiply by one one three,
When three one something four
　　you'll see.

*What number am I?
It helps to work backwards.*

One little frog has two eyes,
Four legs,
One mouth, no tail.
Says croak, croak and
Plops into the water.

Two little frogs have four eyes,
Eight legs,
Two mouths, no tails,
Say croak, croak and
Plop into the water.

*Go on from here.
This is a traditional Chinese rhyme.
You could make up similar rhymes, e.g,
for bees which buzz and fly into the air.*

'Come into my parlour'
Said the spider to the fly.
'Answer now my question
Unless you want to die.
To give me forty-five fly legs –
The number I desire –
How many flies with just five legs
Am I going to require?'

You can vary the numbers of legs.

Shapes

My triangle has three sides.
It stands upon its toes.

But when I gently turn it round,
Down it goes.

My shapely square has four sides,
It stands upon its toes.

But when I gently turn it round,
Down it goes.

I looked in the mirror,
And what did I see?

A p was a q

And a q was a p.

But just the same

Were O and V.

What other letters looked the same?
Did any other letters change places?

I see triangles
Everywhere.
Shark's fins, cheeses,
And bobbing yachts.

I see rectangles
Everywhere.
Window panes, cornflake packs,
And parking lots.

I see circles
Everywhere.
Drinking straws, ends of tins,
And chimney pots.

Where else do you see these shapes?

My kite flies high
Up in the sky.

It turns around
And hits the ground.

It's such a sight –
But still a kite!

You see me in a sunflower.
You see me in a shell.
You see me in a bed spring.
What am I? Can you tell?

Talking points described in full

This section describes some talking points and develops them in full. Links to levels of the curriculum are given but many of the talking points can be adjusted to other levels by varying the range of numbers or shapes used. The questions which you might ask are listed so that they can act as prompts when you are working with the children.

The vocabulary which might be emphasised and any resources needed are both indicated. The resources are those that should be readily available in any primary classroom: for example, dice, straws, counters, coins, calculators, cubes and other shapes, squared paper.

Talking with children is not only a good way to teach; it is also a good way to assess their progress. Some statements of attainment – learning objectives which you could assess – are included in each talking point. Besides these, many of the talking points are intended to encourage children to use and apply mathematics. You could also take the opportunity to assess their skills in this respect – their ability to

> talk about their work;
> ask and respond to questions;
> use and interpret mathematical vocabulary;
> make predictions;
> work systematically;
> explain their methods;
> present their results in a clear and organised way;
> justify their conclusions;
> generalise from a number of particular examples;

and so on. Before you make any assessments, you might like to read pages 29 and 30 on assessing children's achievements.

Counting on

Words to emphasise

One, two, three …
How many?
More, fewer.
Add, take away.
Altogether, total.

You will need

Small cubes, and a
bag or box to hide
them in.

Organisation
This activity works best with a small group.

Talking point
Arrange up to ten cubes on a table and ask a child to count
them. Rearrange them and ask another child to count them.
Confirm that all the children know the number of cubes.

Put all the cubes in a box so that they are hidden. Ask how
many cubes there are in the box. Now take a handful of the
cubes and put them back on the table top. Ask children to say
how many cubes there are on the table. Then ask how many
cubes there must be in the box. Encourage counting on from
the number on the table. Return all the cubes to the box and
take out another handful. Children can take turns to count on.

Questions to ask
- How many cubes are there altogether?
- How many cubes are there on the table?
- How many cubes must there be in the box?
- What if I put five cubes on the table? How many would
  there be in the box?
- What if we had twelve cubes altogether, with five of them on
  the table? How many would there be in the box then?

Follow up for individuals
Record all the different combinations of, say, eight counters.

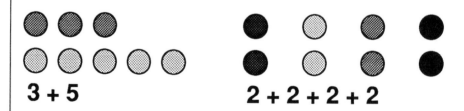

3 + 5   **2 + 2 + 2 + 2**

Assessment: can children
- recognise conservation of number;
- find the difference between two numbers by counting on;
- recognise patterns of numbers which add to a given total?

Two counters

Words to emphasise

One, two, three ...
How many?
More, fewer.
Altogether, total.
Sum, difference.
Plus, minus, equals.
Add, subtract.

You will need

A marker pen.

For a small group, two counters.

For a large group, two large squares of plain white card, and pencil and paper for each child to record answers.

Organisation
This can either be done with a small group with answers given orally, or with a larger group with answers written down.

Talking point
Take two counters and write a different single digit number on each side of each of them. Put the counters on a table and ask the children to give the total of the two numbers which are face up. Then ask questions similar to those below, but before each one, turn over one or both of the counters so that the numbers change. With a bigger group, write large numerals on both sides of two squares of card. Hold them up for children to see.

Examples of questions to ask
• What is the sum of ... and ...?
• Subtract ... from ... What do you get?
• What is ... more than ...?
• How many more than ... is ...?
• Add ... to ... What is the total?
• What is the difference between ... and ...?
• What is ... plus ...?
• What is ... fewer than ...?
• If you count on ... from ..., which number do you get?
• What is ... minus ...? What is ... take away ...?
• How many fewer than ... is ...?
• When I take ... from a number, I get ... What is the number?

Follow up for pairs
What numbers would be on the counters (a) if the totals were 8, 9, 10 and 11; (b) if the differences were 2, 3 and 7?

Assessment: can children
• interpret the language associated with number;
• demonstrate that they know and can use number facts?

What can we buy?

Words to emphasise

Price, cost, value.
Sum, total.
Difference, more, less.
Possibilities.
Most, least.

You will need

For the follow up,
a set of coins.

Organisation

You could start this talking point with a large group, posing appropriate questions to particular children. Ask the children to discuss their answers with a partner before telling you.

Talking point

Arrange about a dozen objects on a table, together with some coins: 1p, 2p, 5p, 10p and 20p. Each object should be labelled clearly with a price up to 10p. For a larger group, stick some pictures and prices on a wall chart. Ask the children what things they might buy and how they would pay.

Questions to ask

- What would we have to pay for the ...? What would we have to pay for the ... and the ...? What would be the total cost of the ..., the ... and the ...?
- What is the difference in price between the ... and the ...? How much more than the ... is the ...?

Choose an amount, say 13p.
- What two things could you buy for exactly 13p? What other possibilities are there?
- Could you buy three things for exactly 13p? Are there any other possibilities?
- What coins could you use to pay exactly 13p? What other possibilities are there? How many different possibilities are there altogether? What is the least number of coins you need?
- If you paid 20p, how much change would you get?

Follow up for pairs

Investigate and record all the different amounts you could pay if you had only one 10p, one 5p, one 2p and one 1p coin.
(1p, 2p, 3p, 5p, 6p, 7p, 8p, 10p, 11p, 12p, 13p, 15p, 16p, 17p, 18p)

Assessment: can children

- recall number bonds to 20;
- choose coins to pay for an item and work out change?

Ribbons

Number

Level 3

Words to emphasise

Estimate.
About, approximately.
Accurate.

Centimetres.

You will need

Twenty different
lengths of ribbon in
different widths.

Pencil and paper for
each child.

For the follow up,
for each pair, a set of
zigzag or wavy lines
drawn on A4 paper.
A ruler marked in
centimetres.
A piece of string.

Organisation
This activity can be carried out with a large group.

Talking point
Get ready a set of about 20 ribbons in different lengths and
widths. Hold up each ribbon in turn and ask the children to
write an estimate of its length.

Questions to ask
- How long do you think this ribbon is? Estimate its length.
- How many of you estimated more than 20 cm?
  Whose estimate was the greatest?
- How many of you estimated less than 20 cm?
  Whose estimate was the least?
- What was the range of estimates?
- This ribbon is 18 cm long. Whose estimate was within 3 cm?
  Whose estimate was within 10 cm?
  Whose estimate was the most accurate?
- How did you judge how long the ribbon was?

Follow up for pairs
Estimate the lengths of lines like these. Check by measuring.

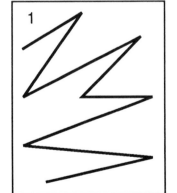 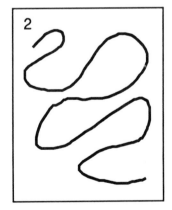

Assessment: can children
- estimate lengths in centimetres and check results;
- use subtraction facts?

Crooked rules

Words to emphasise

Whole number.
Units, tens.
Place, value, digit.

Add, sum, total.
Subtract, difference.

You will need

A dice, preferably large.

A copy of the playing board.

For the follow up, a set of cards numbered 1 to 5, a pencil and some squared paper, and a calculator for each child.

Organisation
Divide children into four teams, with up to three in each team.

Talking point
Draw the playing board shown below. Divide the group into four teams. Roll a 1 to 6 dice for each team in turn. The team will then choose to place the digit rolled in either the units, tens or hundreds column. It can go in the team's own row, or in the row of one of the other teams. Each team should aim to make its own number the smallest.

Team A			
Team B			
Team C			
Team D			

Questions to ask
- What is the best place to put a small digit?
- What is the best place to put a large digit?
- In which place is the …? What is the value of the … in the tens place? Of the … in the hundreds place?
- What if you aimed to make the largest possible number?

Follow up for each team
Use a set of five cards numbered 1 to 5. Arrange the cards to make the answer to a. as large as possible. Then arrange them to make b. as small as possible. Use a calculator to help.

a. ☐ ☐ ☐
+ ☐ ☐

b. ☐ ☐ ☐
– ☐ ☐

Assessment: can children
- recognise place value?

Four in a row

Words to emphasise

Add, subtract,
multiply, divide,
equals.

Plus, minus.

Tens, units.

You will need

A 7 × 6 grid drawn on
the blackboard, filled
randomly with the
numbers 1 to 42.

Chalk in two colours,
one colour for each
team.

Organisation
Divide the whole class into two teams.

Talking point
Allocate a colour to each team. Draw a 7 × 6 grid on the
blackboard and fill it randomly with the numbers 1 to 42.

7	2	28	4	16	6	38
34	20	42	11	33	13	23
40	31	17	5	19	30	21
22	14	24	36	8	27	1
29	39	15	32	12	26	35
25	37	18	3	9	41	10

Explain to the class that they are to make numbers on the grid
using each of the digits 1, 2, 3 and 4 once only, and any of the
operations +, −, ×, ÷. For example,

$$45 = 43 + 2 \times 1$$

Teams should now take turns to make one of the numbers.
When a number is made, cross it through in coloured chalk.
The winning team is the first to get four squares of its own
colour in a line, either horizontally, vertically or diagonally.

Questions to ask
• Which is the best square to aim for now?
• Have you thought of using a different operation?

Follow up for small groups
Which numbers from 1 to 100 can you make using four 4s?

Assessment: can children
• recall and use number bonds and multiplication facts;
• add and subtract mentally two one- or two-digit numbers?

Darts

Words to emphasise

Multiply, product.
Divide.

Add, plus, sum, total.

You will need

A dartboard drawn
on the blackboard or
on a poster.

Organisation
This activity can be carried out with a group of any size.

Talking point
Draw the 'dartboard' on the blackboard. Tell the group that
Karen, Tracey and Dean played darts. Each threw six darts, all
of which hit the board. In some cases, more than one dart hit
the same number, but only one hit the bullseye. Karen and
Tracey both scored 40 in different ways, and Dean scored 30.
What hits did each of them make?

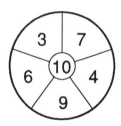

Questions to ask
• What six throws could make 30? (Four 3s, two 9s)
  What could make 40? (Ten, five 6s; two 7s, two 4s, two 9s)
• Are there any other possibilities?
• When two darts hit the same number, this is called a double.
  Three darts on the same number is called a treble. What
  scores are possible with three doubles?   Two trebles?
• If each player threw three darts, and each landed on different
  numbers, what scores would be possible?

Follow up for individuals or pairs
Each number in this table is the
product of the number in the left
column and the number in the top
row.
Can you complete the table?
(Top row: 5, 4, 9, 2. Left col: 2, 3, 7, 1.)

×		4	9	
		8	18	
3		12		
	35			14
				2

Assessment: can children
• recall and use multiplication facts;
• add mentally several single-digit numbers;
• add mentally two two-digit numbers?

What method?

Number

Level 4

Words to emphasise

Add, plus, total, sum.
Multiply, product.
Hundreds, tens, units.

You will need

For the follow up,
pencil and paper.

Organisation
Children can work individually and then share their strategies
with the whole group.

Talking point
Tell the children to work out in their heads 58 + 67. Don't ask
for the answer but ask them how they did it. Did they try to do
what they might do with pencil and paper? Did they count on
60 from 58, and then add 7? Did they round up 58 to 60, add 70
and then subtract 5? Or did they use other methods?

Now ask them to work out in their heads 5 × 26. Then find out
how they did it. Some may have multiplied by 10 and halved
the result. Some may have thought of it as 5 × 20 plus 5 × 6, or
5 × 30 minus 5 × 4, or as 5 × 25 plus 5. Were there other ways?
Emphasise the variety of interesting and acceptable methods.

Questions to ask
- How did you do it?
- What other ways are there?
- Is there a best way of doing it?
- How can you check your result?

Follow up for small groups
- If you could use only these keys on your calculator,

how could you make the numbers 20, 32, 45?
Can you make each of the numbers from 1 to 20?
- Without a calculator, find two numbers with a product of 259.

Assessment: can children
either mentally or with pencil and paper:
- add and subtract two two-digit numbers;
- multiply a two-digit by a one-digit number?

Carrots

Words to emphasise

Add, plus, total, sum.
Tens, units.
Estimate, calculate.
Approximately.

Organisation

Divide into teams. Teams take turns to suggest their ideas, which you might record on a blackboard.

Talking point

Show children the grid below and tell them that a gardener has planted carrots on 16 plots of land. Ask which plots could be dug up to give exactly 100 carrots.

16	43	59	41
25	2	32	11
82	34	57	73
9	64	48	30

Questions to ask

- What is a good way to estimate?
- Does it help to look at the last digits only?
- Does it help to round each number to the nearest ten?
- How many different possibilities are there?
- How could you check your calculations?

Follow up for small groups

Which three plots would give approximately 1000 carrots?
Find as many different combinations as possible.

276	380	81	332
341	644	538	630
575	25	189	93
469	168	438	132

You will need

A 4 x 4 grid filled with two-digit numbers as shown, and large enough for all to see.

For each group for the follow up, a copy of the 4 x 4 grid filled with three-digit numbers. A calculator, and pencil and paper.

Assessment: can children

- estimate numbers which will add to 100 (or 1000);
- add mentally three two-digit numbers;
- add with a calculator three three-digit numbers?

Lemonade

Words to emphasise

Add, subtract, multiply, divide, equals.

Halve, double.

You will need

The calculation
15 × 28 = 420 written on a board.

A picture of a bottle of lemonade marked 28p (optional).

Organisation
This activity can take place with a large group. Children can answer orally or record written answers.

Talking point
Tell the group that Yasmin bought 15 bottles of lemonade at 28p each for her party.

Yasmin had £4.20 ready to pay because she knew that

$$15 \times 28 = 420$$

Write this calculation on the board. Now ask the children to use this information to answer your questions.

Questions to ask
- What is:
    the cost of 16 bottles of lemonade;
    the cost of 30 bottles of lemonade;
    the cost of 15 bottles if they cost 14p each;
    the cost of 15 bottles if they cost 56p each;
    the cost of 15 bottles at 29p each;
    the cost of a packet of crisps if 28 packets cost £4.20?
- Could you answer other questions by using the information?

Follow up for individuals or pairs
What other calculations can you work out if 24 packets of rice at 72p each cost £17.28? Make up more problems like this.

Assessment: can children
- use patterns in existing information to calculate mentally?

Place values

Words to emphasise

Whole number,
decimal, fraction.
Decimal places.
Units, tens, hundreds,
thousands,
tenths, hundredths,
thousandths.

Approximation.
Accuracy.

You will need

A metre stick.

For the follow up,
scissors and old
magazines, glue sticks,
poster paper.

Organisation
You can work with a group of any size, directing appropriate
questions to particular children.

Talking point
Hold up a metre stick. Ask children to name something about
1m in length. Make a note of it. Now ask them to name things
about 10m in length or distance. Build up a table similar to the
one below. Emphasise that as you go up and down the list,
you are multiplying or dividing by 10.

10 000 m	distance to the town centre
1 000 m	from the school to the church
100 m	length of the playground fence
10 m	length of the swimming pool
1 m	length of the metre stick
0.1 m	length of a pencil
0.01 m	width of a thumb nail
0.001 m	thickness of a 20p coin
0.0001 m	thickness of a hair

Now discuss things which are, for example, about 3m (or three
metre sticks) long or 0.04m (four thumb nails) wide, and so on.

Questions to ask
• What is approximately ten times the width of a thumb nail?
• What is one hundredth of the length of a pencil?
• How long is the swimming pool in pencil lengths?
• How many thumb nails will fit along the playground fence?

Follow up in small groups
• Discuss weights or capacities in a similar way.
• Cut out pictures from magazines and label their dimensions.

Assessment: can children
• recognise the relationships between the values of adjacent
  digits in a decimal number;
• make sensible estimates of distances and lengths?

Estimate the number of ...

Words to emphasise

Units, tens, hundreds, thousands, millions.
Estimate.
Degree of accuracy.
Range, greatest, least.
Average.

You will need

For the follow up, some calculators.

Organisation

You can work with a group of any size, directing appropriate questions to particular children.

Talking point

Ask each child to guess how many people could stand comfortably in the classroom. Then ask the group to suggest ways in which the estimate could be made more accurate: for example, making assumptions about how many could stand in a row across the classroom and estimating the number of rows. Pick out from the range of revised estimates the greatest and least estimate and ask what they think the average is. Consider the degree of accuracy: for example, is the estimate likely to be correct to the nearest ten, hundred, thousand, or more?

Questions to ask

- Can you estimate the number of ...?
- How could you make your estimate more accurate?
- What other numbers could you estimate? How could you make each estimate as accurate as possible?
- How accurate is the estimate – is it likely to be to the nearest ten, or hundred, or thousand, or more?
- What numbers can you estimate with reasonable accuracy? What estimates do you feel less confident about? Why?

Follow up for small groups

Ask small groups to choose a large number to estimate: the number of words in a book, leaves on a tree, cornflakes eaten in a year by the class ... Offer a calculator to those who are less confident. More able pupils can make a mental approximation. Ask them to say how accurate their approximate answer is likely to be. At level 5, results might be recorded using index notation.

Assessment: can children

- estimate a number by making an approximate calculation;
- recognise an appropriate degree of accuracy;
- use index notation?

Approximations

Words to emphasise

Divide.
Whole number,
decimal, fraction.
Remainder.
Approximately.
Rounded up,
rounded down.
Decimal places,
tenths, hundredths.
Accuracy.

You will need

For small group work,
pencil and paper to
record stories.

For the follow up, a
calculator for each
child.

Organisation
You can work with a group of any size.

Talking point
Ask how children would work out an approximate answer to
169 ÷ 40. Emphasise that you don't want to know the answer,
just the method. Compare the methods used, which might
include 16 tens divided by 4 tens, or 200 divided by 40.
Discuss whether the answer might be nearer to 4 or nearer to 5.

Ask children to think of some stories to illustrate the division.
If the group is large, stories can be worked on in small groups,
with one member of each group keeping a record for later
feedback to the whole group. Pick out similarities in situations
which require rounding up, and in those which require rounding down.

Questions to ask
- Can you think of a story about 169 ÷ 40 in which the best
  answer would be 4? (For example, *How many 40m rolls of
  chain link fence can be made from a length of 169m?*)
- Can you think of a story about 169 ÷ 40 in which the best
  answer would be 5? (For example, *How many 40m rolls of
  chain link fence are needed to fence a length of 169m?*)
- In what situations would you expect the answer to be more
  accurate? (For example, *A length of 169m of chain link fence is
  cut into 40 equal pieces. How long is each piece?* In this case, it
  would be resonable to expect the answer of 4.225m to be
  accurate to 1cm, or two decimal places, rather than to 1mm.)

Follow up for pairs
One whole number less than 20 divided by another produces
the result 1.5454545 on a calculator. What were the numbers?

Assessment: can children
- approximate, using significant figures;
- recognise when to round remainders up or down?

Sponge prints

Algebra
Level 1

Words to emphasise

First, second, third ...
One, two, three ...

Next to, beside, last,
before, after.

Repeat, pattern.

Names of shapes.

You will need

Aprons for the
children.
Sponges, paint, water.
A long strip of paper
on which the pattern
can be printed.

For the follow up,
copies of the border
pattern and felt-pens
or crayons.
A set of right-angled
triangles in card or
plastic.
Gummed paper
triangles.

Organisation
Work with a small group of children. Within the group, they
might work in pairs.

Talking point
Show the children some sponges and discuss the shapes of the
faces. Tell the children that they are going to print a pattern
along a strip of paper. They might use two different sponges,
one in each hand, or one sponge, changing the face each time,
or they might have other ideas.

Questions to ask
• What pattern shall we make? What shapes shall we use?
  What colours shall we use?
• Can you describe the pattern to me?
• What is the fourth shape in your pattern?
• What shape comes after the third yellow shape?

Follow up for individuals or pairs
• Colour this border using a repeated sequence of colours.

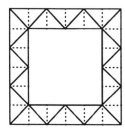

• Make a copy of the border pattern using sets of right-angled
  triangles or gummed paper triangles.

Assessment: can children
• recognise common two-dimensional shapes;
• use vocabulary to describe position;
• devise and extend a repeating pattern?

Block patterns

Words to emphasise

In front, behind, next to, before, after, above, under, right, left.

One, two, three ...
Red, yellow, blue ...
Names of shapes.

Balance, symmetry.
Mirror image.
Flip, turn.

You will need

Cards illustrating some block patterns.

A set of blocks.

A mirror.

For the follow up, blocks or counters, questions on worksheets.

Organisation
Work with a small group of children.

Talking point
Provide a set of wooden blocks for children to use to build the pattern on each card. They can build at the side of the card or build from memory by turning the card over before starting. A mirror placed at an edge can be used to show a reflection

Explore ways of building the pattern and of recording the numbers that it symbolises.

Questions to ask
- Which pattern do you like best? Can you describe it to me?
- Build the pattern. What blocks did you use? What colours did you use? How many red ones did you use?
- Can you describe your pattern using numbers: for example, $2 + 2 + 1 = 5$?
- This pattern uses five blocks, two red and three blue. How else could we use five red or blue blocks to make a pattern?
- Besides $2 + 3$, what other patterns for five are there?
- If you repeat this pattern, how many blocks will you use?

Follow up for individuals
- Find the missing numbers.
$$3 + \blacksquare = 10$$
$$\blacksquare + 2 = 7$$
- Suggest numbers that fit into:
$$\blacktriangle + \blacktriangle = \blacklozenge$$

Assessment: can children
- use patterns in addition and subtraction facts to 10;
- recognise that a symbol stands for an unknown number?

Coins

Algebra

Levels 2, 3

Words to emphasise

One, two, three ...
Values of coins.
Sum, total.
Pattern.
Combination.
Odd, even.

You will need

Coins.

For the follow up,
coins, pencil and
paper for each pair.

Organisation
A group of about six children is best for this activity.

Talking point
Put one 10p piece, one 5p, one 2p and one 1p on the table top.

Ask the children what different amounts they could pay by using just the coins on the table.

Questions to ask
- What coins will you use? What is their total value?
- How shall I keep a record?
- Is 1p + 2p + 5p the same as or different from 2p + 1p + 5p?
- What is the smallest amount you can make? What is the largest?
- Which odd numbers can you make? Which even numbers can you make? Is it easier to make odd numbers or even numbers? Why do you think so?
- Can you make 14p? Why not?
- How many different totals have you found so far?
- Have you found all the different ways? How do you know?
- Can you see any patterns?

Follow up for individuals or pairs
Record all the different ways of:
- making 25p using only 5p and 10p coins; (3 ways)
- making 50p using only 5p, 10p and 20p coins. (12 ways)

Assessment: can children
- add mentally pairs of small numbers;
- distinguish odd and even numbers;
- use patterns of numbers to work systematically?

Squares

Words to emphasise

First, second, third …
Add, total.

Rule, formula.

Organisation
This activity is best carried out sitting round a table with a group of up to six children.

Talking point
Put out this pattern on the table top.

Ask the children to describe the pattern and to say how it would continue.

Questions to ask
- Can you describe this pattern?
  Is there another way of describing it?
- How many squares are needed to make each shape?
- Can you predict the number of squares needed to make the next shape? What reasons do you have?
- How many squares would be needed for the 10th shape?
  How do you know?
- Can you say in your own words what the rule is for finding the number of squares needed for any shape in the pattern?

You will need

Plenty of squares or cubes to represent the pattern.

For the follow up, squared paper.

Follow up with the group
- Can you answer similar questions about this pattern?

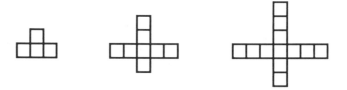

- Make up your own pattern. Write a description of it.

Assessment: can children
- explain a number pattern and predict subsequent numbers;
- recognise multiples of three and four;
- make general statements about patterns?

Algebra

Counters

Words to emphasise

First, second, third ...
Multiply, divide.
Remainder.

Proportion, ratio.

Probability.

You will need

Counters in two
colours.

For the follow up,
pencil and paper.

Organisation
This activity is best carried out sitting round a table with a
group of up to six children at a similar level of attainment.

Talking point
Put out this pattern of red and blue counters on the table top.

Ask the children to confirm how the pattern would continue.
Then ask questions like those listed below.

Questions to ask
- Can you describe the pattern?
- What colour is the 4th counter ... or the 15th ... or the 44th?
  Make some more questions like this.
- In what position is the 7th red counter ... or the 15th blue
  counter? Make up more questions like this.
- If there were 50 counters altogether in the pattern, how many
  red ones would there be? How do you know?
- If there were 31 blue counters in the pattern, how many red
  ones would there be? How do you know?
- If there were 23 counters in the pattern, what proportion
  would be red? What would be the ratio of red to blue
  counters? If I put them all in a bag, then picked out one,
  what would be the probability of it being blue?

Follow up for pairs
Children can work in pairs to create similar problems for other
pairs to work on. They should also prepare answers. The
initial patterns can be drawn on paper or laid out on a table.

Assessment: can children
- explain a number pattern and predict how it would continue;
- make general statements about patterns;
- use patterns when doing mental calculations;
- interpret the meanings of ratio, proportion, probability?

Shape sequence

Straight, edge, parallel.

Angle, acute, obtuse, reflex, right angle, degrees.

Top, bottom, left, right. Reflect, slide, translate.

Names of shapes.

Coordinates, quadrant.

A sketch of the pattern on a card, one card for each pair of children. A large thin book to act as a screen. Pencil and paper.

For the follow up, squared paper, pencil and a ruler for each child.

Organisation
Within a larger group, children should work in pairs.

Talking point
Prepare a sketch of this pattern on a card. You will need one card for each pair of children working on the task.

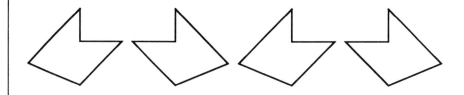

Each pair should have a screen placed between them. One child is given the card but keeps it hidden from the other. The first child describes the pattern to the other – without any movement of the hands to indicate angles, directions or lengths! The second child tries to reproduce the pattern. Since there are many different ways of describing the pattern, the activity might culminate in a sharing with the whole group.

Questions to ask
- How did you describe the basic shape?
  How else could you describe it?
- How did you describe the pattern?
- If the basic shape were plotted, what might the coordinates of its vertices be?

Follow up for pairs
- Draw the shape in the first quadrant. Label its vertices with coordinates. If the shape were reflected in the horizontal axis, what would the coordinates of the reflection be?
- What if it were reflected in the vertical axis?

Assessment: can children
- recognise movements such as reflection or translation;
- use properties of shapes to justify explanations;
- specify location;
- use coordinates?

Greetings

Words to emphasise

Pointed, curved, wavy, rounded, straight, edge, corner, zig-zag, sloping.

Top, bottom, under, over, right, left, corner.

Turn, slide, fit.

You will need

Old greetings cards cut into not too many interesting shapes, one card for each pair of children.

For the follow up, more old cards and some scissors.

Organisation
Within a larger group, children should work in pairs.

Talking point
Take the picture from an old greetings card, one for each pair of children. Cut the picture into not too many pieces, using wavy or zig-zag lines to make interesting shapes. Give the shuffled pieces to a pair of children, who should sit side by side at a table. One child, who must not touch the pieces, gives instructions to enable the other child to complete the 'jig-saw'.

Questions to ask
- What might the picture be? Tell me about it.
- How many pieces are there? How many have corners?
- How could you sort the pieces?
- What other ways of sorting the pieces are there?
- What pieces would fit in the corner ... or go round this point?
- What sort of edge would fit here?

Follow up for pairs
Give the children another old card each, a pencil and some scissors, to make another jigsaw. They can then shuffle the pieces and give them to a partner to put together again. More able children might be given two cards shuffled together.

Assessment: can children
- use words like straight, flat, curved, round, pointed;
- fit one shape to another;
- give or follow instructions on movement or position?

Shapes from cubes

Shape and space

Levels 1, 2

Words to emphasise

One, two, three ...

Straight, long, short, edge, corner, end, top, bottom, left, right, above, below, under, over, beside.

Red, yellow, blue ...

You will need

Cubes that snap together (for example, Multilink).
Large thin books to act as screens.

For the follow up, copies of the diagrams.

Organisation
This activity works well with a group of up to six children.

Talking point
You need some cubes that lock together, such as Multilink, and a large book to make a screen between you and the children. Place a few cubes on your own side of the screen and the rest on the children's side. To demonstrate, make a shape from three or four cubes. Keep it hidden. Explain how you made your shape, cube by cube, so that the children can make one exactly the same as yours. For example: *Take a green cube. Put a second green cube on top of it. Put a yellow cube to the right of the top green cube. Put a red cube behind the yellow cube.* When they have finished, the children can compare their cubes with yours.

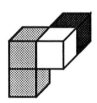

Questions to ask
• Are the shapes the same? If not, how are they different?
• On my shape, which cube is in front of the red cube?
• If I turn the shape like this, where is the yellow cube now?

Follow up for pairs
• Children can continue by working in pairs, one making an interesting hidden shape for the other to replicate.
• For further follow up, children could construct the shapes shown in diagrams like those below.

   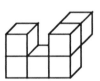

Assessment: can children
• recognise the position of one object relative to another;
• visualise and describe shapes made from cubes?

Peek-a-boo

Shape and space

Levels 1, 2

Words to emphasise

Pointed, curved, rounded, straight, edge, corner, slope, end, top, bottom.

Concave, convex.

Names of shapes.

Right angle.

You will need

Assorted 2D shapes, including crescents, semicircles, stars. Large thin books to act as screens.

For the follow up, pencil and paper. A worksheet of hidden shapes.

Organisation
This activity works best with a group of about six children, so that they do not have to wait too long between turns.

Talking point
You need a box of assorted flat shapes and a large book to make a screen between you and the children. Choose a shape without letting the children see it, and show a tiny part of it above the screen, perhaps a corner or an edge. Ask children to take turns to guess what the shape might be. Each time anyone makes a guess, they must say why they think it might be such a shape before being told yes or no. After each guess, take the shape down behind the screen and turn it so that a different part is shown. Children can carry on, working in pairs.

Questions to ask
• What might the shape be? Why do you think that?
• What other shape could it be?

Follow up for pairs or individuals
• One child might draw a picture of a hidden shape from a verbal description given by the other.
• Draw and label all the shapes used.
• Complete the shapes hidden behind screens on a worksheet.

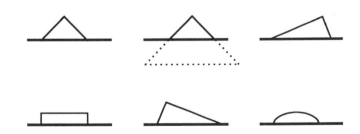

Assessment: can children
• use mathematical terms to describe properties of 2D shapes;
• recognise right-angled corners?

Treasure hunt

Words to emphasise

Compass directions.

You will need

A map divided into squares drawn on a poster or blackboard.

Alternatively, provide each small group with the map drawn on a worksheet.

Organisation

This activity can be carried out with a large group with the map drawn on a blackboard, or in small groups, using a worksheet, with time to discuss the possibilities in the group.

Talking point

Sketch a map similar to the one below on a blackboard. Indicate which direction is north.

Give clues to the group. As they respond, the features can be marked on the map until the treasure is found. Emphasise that only one feature is located in each 'square'.

Clues to give
- The swamp is north-west of the giant frog.
- The frog is north-east of the camp.
- The tree and the lake are north-west of the sand dunes.
- The old shack is south-west of the tree and east of the cliffs.
- The tree is north-east of the caves and west of the forest.
- The grave is east of the hill and north-west of the gallows.
- The treasure is between the camp and the look out post.

Follow up for small groups
- Write the clues as if north were to the bottom of the map.
- Make a similar problem for another group to solve.

Assessment: can children
- use the eight compass directions?

Tangrams

Shape and space

Levels 3, 4

Words to emphasise

Up, down, top, bottom, left, right, above, below. Right angle, 45°. Turn, rotate. Flip, reflect. Slide, translate.

Names of shapes.

You will need

For each pair, a set of tangram shapes, and a tangram picture card.

Organisation
Children should work in pairs, sitting side by side at a table.

Talking point
Tangram shapes can be made from a square cut into 7 pieces.

Make cards, each with a picture made from the tangram pieces.

One child should take a card, hiding it from his or her partner. Without touching any of the pieces, this child should give instructions to enable the other to assemble the picture. Once complete, the arrangement can be compared with the picture on the card. More able pairs of children might be asked to give instructions to make the mirror image of the picture.

Questions to ask
• Where should that piece go in relation to this one?
• How can that piece be moved into the right position – should it be rotated or reflected? Through 90° or through 45°?
• How far should you slide that piece?
• Can you give instructions to make the mirror image?
• How are instructions best worded to be really helpful?

Follow up for individuals
Create more pictures using the tangram pieces.

Assessment: can children
• give instructions on orientation or position;
• construct shapes from given information?

Overlaps

Words to emphasise

Pointed, curved, rounded, straight, edge, side, vertex.

Turn, rotate.
Flip over, reflect.
Slide.

Names of shapes.
Equilateral, isosceles, right angled, scalene.

You will need

Shapes to demonstrate with, preferably transparent. Alternatively, sketch the shapes on the blackboard.

For the follow up, for each pair, two card squares, tracing paper, scissors, plain paper and pencil.

Organisation
This activity can be carried out with a medium sized group.

Talking point
Take a rectangle and a triangle. Show the children one placed over the other. This is best demonstrated with transparent film, placed on an overhead projector if the group is large, or with shapes drawn on tracing paper. Tell the children that when two shapes overlap each other, a third shape is made.

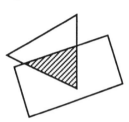

Ask the children to close their eyes and imagine two equilateral triangles. Think how to overlap the triangles to make a triangle, rhombus, hexagon … Are there different ways of doing it?

Questions to ask
- How could two equilateral triangles overlap to make another equilateral triangle? Are there other ways of doing it?
- What other types of triangle could you make?
- What if you rotate, reflect or slide the top triangle?
- Can you make an overlap shape with four sides? A different shape with four sides? A shape with five sides? Six sides?
- What if the two triangles were right angled?
- What if we used a rectangle and a triangle?

Follow up for pairs
- What overlap shapes can you make with two squares?
- How could this pattern be made?
- Can you program a turtle to make it?

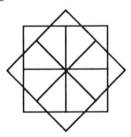

Assessment: can children
- construct 2D shapes and recognise their properties;
- use turtle graphics instructions for distance and direction?

Pentominoes

Words to emphasise

Above, below.
Left, right.
Line of symmetry.
Area, perimeter.

You will need

A pencil and squared
paper for each child.

For the follow up,
squared paper,
felt pens.

Organisation
This activity can be undertaken with a large group.

Talking point
Ask everyone to draw secretly a pentomino – a shape made
from five squares touching edge to edge. They should then
turn over the paper and take turns to describe their shapes for
the rest of the group to draw. Afterwards, they can compare
drawings to see how accurately they have communicated.

Questions to ask after all the shapes are drawn
• How many of the pentominoes are symmetrical?
• What is the area of each pentomino? What is the perimeter?
• Which pentominoes are the same? Which are different?
• Have all the possible pentominoes been drawn?
  How many different possibilities are there? (12)
• Which two pentominoes could fit into this shape? How
  would you arrange them? Can you find four different pairs?

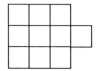

Follow up for individuals
Which of the 12 pentomino shapes will tessellate? (All 12)
Draw and colour some tessellations. Find the area coloured.

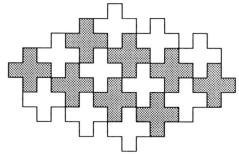

Assessment: can children
• recognise properties such as symmetry or ability to tessellate;
• recognise that shapes of the same area may have different
  perimeters;
• find the area or perimeter of simple shapes;
• use multiples of five?

Jigsaws

Words to emphasise

Above, below, next to, between.
Left, right.
Flip, turn, slide.
Rotate, reflect.
Clockwise, anticlockwise.

Area, perimeter.

Factors.

You will need

Copies of the jigsaws drawn on a large poster, or alternatively on a worksheet to be shared between a pair of children.

For the follow up, squared paper.

Organisation
This activity can be undertaken with a group of any size.

Talking point
The pieces of the jigsaw are made from the same square with dimples and pimples of the same size cut out or stuck on. Ask children to comment on the total number of pieces, the number of middle pieces, numbers of pimples and dimples, the area of pieces, the shape and perimeter of the jigsaw, any symmetry ...

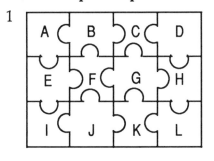
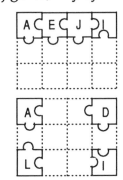

Questions to ask
- Can you rearrange the first jigsaw to make jigsaws 2 or 3?
- Can you make a fourth jigsaw with pieces from the first?
- Can you make a 6 × 2 jigsaw with the pieces? Why not?
- What different shaped rectangular jigsaws could you make with 36 pieces? Which would have the shortest perimeter? Could you make different rectangular jigsaws with 31 pieces?
- How many pimples and dimples on a 3 × 4 jigsaw? On a 5 × 4 jigsaw? On an $n \times m$ jigsaw? (There are $2 \times \{n(m-1) + m(n-1)\}$ on an $n \times m$ jigsaw.)

Follow up for pairs
- How many different corner pieces are possible in a jigsaw? How many with one straight edge? With no straight edge? Which six pieces are not used in the first jigsaw?
- Design a jigsaw using all the 18 possible different pieces.
- Investigate the pieces required for L-shaped jigsaws.

Assessment: can children
- use properties of shapes or numbers to justify explanations;
- express a simple formula in symbolic form?

Symmetrical shapes

Words to emphasise

Line of symmetry,
point of symmetry.

Reflect, rotate.
Clockwise,
anticlockwise.

You will need

Pencil and squared
paper for each pair of
children.

Organisation
Introduce the activity to the whole group but continue by
working in pairs.

Talking point
Show the children a picture of these three shapes. Ask them to
imagine the pieces arranged in a symmetrical shape.

The children should then take turns to describe their shapes to
a partner. After the verbal description, each pair might keep a
record on squared paper.

Questions to ask
- Can you describe your shape to your partner?
- Did you turn round one of the shapes (rotate it)? Did you
  turn one over (reflect it)?
- What other symmetrical shapes can you make?
- Which have line symmetry?
- Which have rotational symmetry?
- How many different possibilities are there?
- What do you do to check whether each shape is new or a
  repeat of a previous one?

Follow up for small groups
- On squared paper, how many different shapes can you make
  from six squares that touch edge to edge? (35)
- How many have line symmetry? (10)
- How many have rotational symmetry? (7)
- How many could be folded to make a cube? (10)

Assessment: can children
- construct 2D shapes;
- recognise reflective and rotational symmetry?

Straw shapes

Words to emphasise

Acute, obtuse, right angled.
Side, vertex, adjacent, opposite.
Parallel, diagonal.

Names of quadrilaterals: square, rectangle, trapezium, rhombus, kite, parallelogram.

Names of triangles: scalene, isosceles, equilateral, right angled.

You will need

Straws in three different lengths.
Pencil and plain paper.

Organisation
This activity can be undertaken with a whole class.

Talking point
Ask the children to imagine that they have some straws. There are just two lengths: short or long. Ask them to 'make' a quadrilateral. They should then describe their quadrilateral to a partner by making as many statements as they can about it. For example, *It's a square. All four sides are short. All four angles are right angles. The opposite sides are parallel. Its diagonals cross at right angles.* Then ask them if they can use the straws to 'make' a different shape of the same type. For example, a large square could be made from four long straws.

Children at level 3 should be able to make different squares/rectangles; those working at level 5 should be able to construct and name the whole set of different quadrilaterals.

Questions to ask
- What is your shape called? What are its special properties?
- Could it also be another shape? (For example, a square also fulfils the definition of a rhombus.)
- Could you make another of those shapes using different straws? Or another . . . ?
- How many different types of quadrilateral can you make?

Follow up for individuals
- Level 3: Using straws of two different lengths, how many different triangles can you make?
- Level 4: Using straws of three different lengths, how many different triangles can you make?
- Level 5: Using straws of three different lengths, how many different quadrilaterals can you make?

Record all the different shapes made on plain paper.

Assessment: can children
- construct triangles and quadrilaterals;
- use properties of shapes to justify explanations?

Fold and cut

Shape and space

Level 5

Words to emphasise

Line of symmetry, reflection.
Point of symmetry, rotation.
Congruence.

Names of shapes, side, vertex.

Right angle, degrees, hypotenuse.

You will need

A stock of thin paper squares, or A4 paper.

A pair of scissors for each child.

Organisation
Children should carry out the practical activity individually.

Talking point
Ask each child to take a piece of paper and fold it to make a straight line. Now fold the line along itself to make a right angle. Cut off a piece by making a straight cut across the right angle. Ask what shape the piece will be before it is unfolded. If they are uncertain, it may help them to consider how many layers of paper they have.

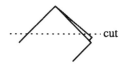

Start again with another piece of paper but this time fold once more to eight thicknesses to make 45°. Try these cuts.

Questions to ask
- Can you describe your shape before unfolding?
- Can you say anything about the properties of the shape (for example, number of sides, whether these are the same length, size of any angles . . .)?
- Does your shape have symmetry? If so, how many lines of symmetry does it have? Does it have rotational symmetry?
- How many congruent triangles are there? How do you know they are congruent?
- How could you fold and cut to make a square? A rhombus? A regular octagon?

Follow up for individuals
Can you fold and cut to make an eight-pointed star?

Assessment: can children
- identify symmetries;
- recognise congruent triangles?

Wheels

Shape and space

Level 6

Words to emphasise

Circle, centre, radius, diameter, circumference, arc, sector.

Semicircle, quadrant.

You will need

For the follow up, a copy of the spiral for each child.
A sharp pencil and plain paper.
Compasses, ruler, set square.

Organisation
Work with a small group at the same level of attainment.

Talking point
Ask the children to close their eyes and imagine they are riding a bike. Ahead they see a long strip of wet yellow paint, 10 cm wide, across the road. They ride across in a straight line.

Questions to ask
• Look back. What marks do you see on the road?
• What if you rode across in a tightly curved line?
• What marks would you see if the distance between the centres of your wheels were greater?
• What would the distance between the centres of the wheels need to be to make the marks from each wheel coincide?
• What if you were riding a tricycle?
• What if you were riding a penny farthing?

Follow up for individuals

• Construct this spiral. It is made from circular arcs. The smallest square is 1 cm × 1 cm.

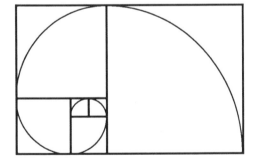

• Calculate the length of the spiral. $(10 \times \pi)$

Assessment: can children
• use accurate measurement and drawing for construction;
• use the formula $C = 2\pi r$ to find the circumference of a circle?

Buttons

Organisation
A small group of up to four children might work on the task.

Talking point
Spread about 50 buttons on a table top. Ask the children what they notice about the buttons. They might mention the colour, size, shape, material, number of holes, and so on. Ask them if they put, say, the red buttons together, what they will do with those that are left over.

Words to emphasise

One, two, three ...

Colours, textures, shapes, materials ...

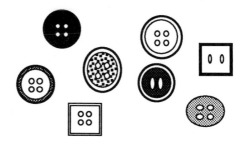

Now ask the children to sort the buttons into piles. Encourage them to think of their own reasons (criteria) for sorting.

Questions to ask
- How did you group your buttons?
- Why did you put these buttons here? And here?
- Could you have put this button here? Why not?
- How many buttons in this group?
- Are there more red buttons or more yellow buttons?
- If I mix up the buttons, what else besides their colour (or whatever criterion the children have used) could you tell me about the buttons?
- How else could you group them?

You will need

A collection of about 50 assorted buttons.

For the follow up, a baseline drawn on a large sheet of paper. Plain paper, a pencil and felt pens or crayons for each child.

Follow up for the group
Children can line up their sets of buttons on a common base line drawn on a large sheet of paper, then draw their 'graph'.

Assessment: can children
- sort according to similarities and differences in colour, shape, texture, size ... and describe their criteria?

Story endings

Handling data

Levels 1, 2 and 3

Words to emphasise

Likely, unlikely,
certain, uncertain,
possible, impossible.
Always, sometimes,
never.

You will need

A short story.

For the follow up,
art media.

Organisation
You can work with a group of any size.

Talking point
Read a short story to the children. Stop half way through and
discuss what possible endings it might have (level 1), what
endings would be impossible, and why (level 2), what is the
most likely/least likely ending, and why (level 3). If the group
is large, children can discuss story endings in smaller groups.

Once upon a time …

Questions to ask
- How do you think the story will end?
- What could be possible? What makes you think that?
- Are you sure about that? Is it certain? Why?
- Would it always happen or just sometimes?
- Would it be fair or unfair? Why do you think so?
- What other possible endings are there? Which one is the
  most likely/least likely? Why?
- What could never happen? What events would be
  impossible in the story? Why?

Follow up for individuals
Illustrate the various endings of the story, labelling them
possible, impossible, certain, uncertain.

Assessment: can children
- recognise possible outcomes and their degree of certainty;
- place events in order of relative likelihood;
- use simple vocabulary associated with probability?

Choosing toys

Words to emphasise

One, two, three ...

Colours, textures,
shapes, materials ...

Same, different.

You will need

A collection of about
12 toys: for example,
bricks, felt pens, a
teddy ...
or pictures of toys
on cards.

A counter.

For the follow up, a
tree diagram on A1
paper, or a suitable
computer program.

Organisation
This activity is best with a small group of up to six children.

Talking point
- Put about a dozen toys where all the group can see them.
  Pick up two toys and ask the children to suggest similarities
  or differences between them. Do this several times.
- Replace the toys and pick up just one: for example, the
  bricks. Say: *I am taking this because it is the only toy you can
  build with.* Children should then take turns to take a toy and
  say what is unique about it. Invite comment each time.
- Hide a counter underneath one toy while children close their
  eyes. They then ask questions to which you only reply *Yes* or
  No. For example, *Is it a toy with arms or legs?*

Questions to ask
- What is the same/different about these two toys?
- Why did you choose that toy? What is special about it?
- What is the same about all the toys that are left?

Follow up for small groups
Children can sort the toys on a prepared tree diagram, or they
can use a suitably prepared computer program.

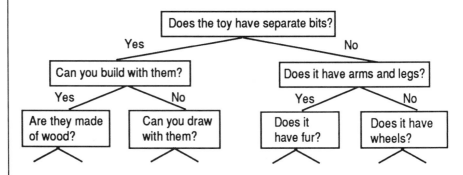

At level 4, children could create their own tree to sort the toys.

Assessment: can children
- choose criteria for sorting and classifying objects;
- use a simple tree diagram to represent results;
- create a decision tree with questions to identify objects?

Opinion poll

Words to emphasise

Information, data.
Survey, opinion poll.
Questionnaire.
Database.

You will need

Catalogues of story
tapes, plants ...

For the follow up,
pencil and paper.
A suitable computer
database.

Organisation
Work with a group of any size, directing appropriate questions
towards particular children.

Talking point
Should the school have a library of story tapes (or a garden
area or a parents' room ...) and, if so, what should be in it?

Questions to ask
- What information should we collect?
- How should possible items for the library be chosen? Free
  choice or choice from a list? If from a list, how should it be
  created?
- How should opinions be collected? By interview or through
  a questionnaire? What are the advantages or disadvantages
  of each method?
- Who should be included in the poll (children, staff, parents,
  governors)? How many of each group should be asked – all,
  or just some? If just some, how should they be chosen?
- Should age be taken into account?
  If so, how should the age of adults be noted?
- Are girls and boys likely to have different views?
  If so, how should these be taken into account?
- How should results be analysed? What kind of outcomes
  would result in deciding for or against a story tape library?
- How and to whom should results be presented?

Follow up for the whole group
- Design a data collection sheet, carry out the survey and
  make a presentation of results.
- Collect examples of published opinion polls from newspapers and mount them in a wall display. Interpret and
  comment on the results.

Assessment: can children
- plan and conduct a survey;
- enter, interrogate and interpret information in a database;
- construct and interpret graphs and frequency diagrams?

Flags

Words to emphasise

Vertical.
Left, right, middle.
Possibilities, outcomes.
Probability.

Organisation
Organise children into ability groups of four.

Talking point
Ask the children to imagine a flag with three vertical stripes, one red, one white and one blue. Children in each group should then take turns to describe their flags to each other. Ask whether their imaginary flags were the same or different.

Now ask them to imagine another flag, one nobody has thought of. Describe these new flags. Ask them, as a group, to decide how many different flags they could make altogether.

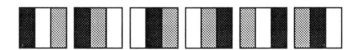

Ask able pupils who finish quickly how many different flags could be made if each colour may be used more than once. (27)

Questions to ask
• Were your imaginary flags different? If so, how?
• How many different flags could you make altogether?
• How can you be sure you have thought of them all?
• What if you could use each colour more than once?

You will need

For the follow-up, paper, felt pens and scissors.
An open box.

Follow up for small groups
Make a set of the six flags and put them in a box. Take a flag. Is the red stripe in the middle? Replace the flag, shuffle them up and try again. Keep repeating this. Record what happens. What is the probability that the flag taken out has a red stripe in the middle? Does it approach the expected probability of two in six, or one-third? Compare with other groups.

Assessment: can children
• list all the possible outcomes of an event;
• calculate a probability based on equally likely outcomes;
• recognise that different outcomes can result from repeating an experiment;
• estimate a probability based on statistical evidence?

Sweet shop

Words to emphasise

Average, mean, mode. Minimum, maximum, range.

You will need

Packets labelled 'average contents' or 'minimum contents'. Plenty of counters. A stop watch.

For the follow up, examples from which to calculate the mean and range.

Small packets to investigate. Pencil and paper.

Organisation
Six children can work together on this activity.

Talking point
Look at some packets labelled *average contents*: for example, a box of matches or a packet of small sweets. What does *average contents* mean? How does it compare with *minimum contents*?

Simulate a production process which requires each person to pack 10 bags, each containing exactly 20 sweets, in one minute. Start with 500 counters to act as 'sweets'. Sort them into piles. Score one penalty point for each pile with more or fewer than 20 sweets. Score five penalty points for each pile not done.

Play again, scoring one penalty point for each pile with more than 20 sweets, three penalty points for each pile with fewer than 20, plus three penalty points for each pile not done.

Questions to ask
- How are small items counted into each box at a factory?
- What was the mean number of 'sweets' in your piles? What was the most common number? What was the range?
- What would you expect the smallest and largest number of matches to be in a new box labelled *minimum contents 200*?
- Why don't manufacturers put an exact number in a packet?
- What are the problems of packaging and selling small items from the manufacturer's point of view?

Follow up for individuals
- Calculate the average contents, and give a range for what you think the maximum and minimum contents might be: for example, 7000 toffees packed in 16 bags.
- Investigate the average contents of small items sold by weight: for example, sweets, nails, things to nibble ...

Assessment: can children
- use the mean and range of a set of data;
- design and use an observation sheet to collect data;
- construct and interpret frequency diagrams?

More ideas

Often you will use your own ideas, or those of the children, as a starting point for discussion. Talk will arise naturally during the everyday life of the school. Classroom organisation and daily routines offer many possibilities for talking and asking questions: for example, tidying up involves sorting objects, arranging things in order or deciding what will fit where. The collection of money or the taking of registers involves counting and classifying. Out-of-school visits and other school events might require the use of timetables, or planning and budgeting. The school buildings and grounds provide opportunities to estimate and measure heights, lengths and areas, to consider plans and work on scale drawings, to look for shapes, patterns or symmetry in brick work, paving or windows.

Other opportunities can arise in a range of subjects across the curriculum. Topics in science, history and geography will, almost certainly, involve the collection, interpretation and presentation of data, some of which will arise from taking measurements. Technology requires measuring, and consideration of two- and three-dimensional shapes, rigidity, size and scale. Cooking can involve measures of weight, capacity and time, the use of fractions and ratio and proportion. Most physical education lessons will require thinking about position, direction, movement, or measures of distance and height, time and speed. Art and design will include work on two- and three-dimensional shapes, patterns, symmetry, reflection and rotation, tessellations, angle, and so on.

The last section of this book sets out briefly some ideas for further talking points linked to a common mathematical theme: for example, doubles and halves. The suggestions within each theme are grouped together so that you can identify easily whether the main purpose of the talking point is to develop vocabulary, to practise mental arithmetic or to use imagery.

The talking points in each group are arranged very roughly in order of difficulty and are related to levels of the curriculum. Where a range of levels is indicated, the exact level is generally dependent on the size and type of number chosen. Solutions to some of the less standard problems are given in brackets at the end of the problem but if children cannot suggest a solution after discussion with their peers or with you, you should not reveal it. Ask them to leave the problem, either temporarily or permanently, knowing that is what real mathematicians do. It took many tens of years to prove that if a map is to be coloured so that adjacent countries are different, then only four colours are needed!

Ordering and place value

| Number | Vocabulary |

Level 1

Vocabulary

- *One, two, three ...*
  How far can you count forwards? What about backwards?
  Count these cubes as I point slowly. Count as I point quickly.
  Count silently while I clap – first spaced evenly, then unevenly.
  I am going to sing two notes: doh and me. Count to yourself the
  number of dohs that I sing.

    doh, doh, doh, me, me, me, doh, doh, doh, me, me, me ...
    doh, me, me, doh, doh, doh, doh, me, doh, me, me, doh ...

Level 1

- *First, second, third ...*
  Look at this string of beads. Point to the third one. What colour
  is the sixth bead? What position is the second yellow bead?
  Which bead comes one before the third red bead? Two after the
  second green bead?

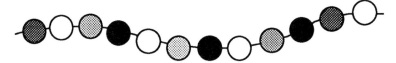

Levels 1, 2

- What number is on your front door, on the bus which stops
  outside the school, on your telephone ...? Where else do you
  see numbers?

Levels 2, 3 and 4

- *Units, tens, hundreds, thousands, millions.*
  Tenths, hundredths, thousandths.
  How far can you count in tens, or hundreds, or thousands?
  How do we say these numbers: 10 070, 2006, 5.0015, 50 015?
  How do we write two thousand and seventeen? One hundred
  and three thousand and sixty?

Levels 3, 4 and 5

- In the number 273, which is the units digit, the tens digit, the
  hundreds digit? In the number 27 300, what is the value of the
  two? Of the seven? Of the three?
  What is the value of the two, seven and three in these numbers:

    a. 2.73   b. 0.0273   c. 27 300 000?

Number	• What words have numbers hidden in them? For example, *ace, uniform, diplomat, biceps, tripod, squadron, quintuplet, punch, sextant, semester, September, sennight, octopus, nonagon, tithe, dozen, hussar, score, quarantine* … What others do you know?
Levels 4, 5	
Level 5	• What meanings are given to *one billion* in the United States and in Britain? What is a *googol*? A good dictionary will help!

Mental arithmetic

Level 2	• How old are you? How old were you last year? How old will you be ten years from now?
Level 2	• Using the digit 1 six times, and as many + signs as you like, can you make the number 15?
Levels 2, 3	• The answer is 10. What is the question?
Level 3	• What is 36 + 10? 36 + 50? What is 26 – 10? 86 – 50?
Level 3	• A quick way to add on 9 is to add on 10 and subtract 1. Start at 0. Count round the class in nines. Now start with a small whole number. How would you change this strategy to count back in nines? What would you do to add or subtract 19?
Levels 3, 4	• What is the cost of 10 crayons at 6p each? 100 crayons? 1000? What is the cost of one cotton reel if they sell at £20 per 100? What if they were £20 per 1000?
Levels 3, 4	• Estimate the number of children in the class to the nearest 10, in the school to the nearest 100, in the town to the nearest 1000.

Ordering and place value

Number

Levels 3, 4

- A bag of 100 coins is worth £1.54 and is made up of 1p and 10p coins. How many of each coin are there? (6 tens and 94 ones)

Level 4

- Two numbers have the same two digits, but in a different order. The difference between them is 45. What could they be? (16 and 61, or 27 and 72, or 38 and 83, or 49 and 94)

Level 4

- To number from 1 the pages of a book, 555 digits were used. How many pages are there? (221) How many 5s were used? (42)

Level 4

- Start at 0. Count round the class adding 0.2 each time. Now try adding 0.05. Try subtracting 0.2 or 0.05. If it's difficult, do the same thing with a calculator to see how the trailing zeros disappear.

Level 4

- If you used only these keys on your calculator,

    $\boxed{1}$ $\boxed{0}$ $\boxed{+}$ $\boxed{=}$ $\boxed{\cdot}$

    how could you make 0.12, 2.4, 0.88, 1.04, 2.21...?

Level 4

- To multiply by 5, multiply by 10 and halve. What is:

    a. 5×28 b. 160×5 c. 17×5?

Level 5

- The scale on a plan drawing is 100 to 1. What is the real length of a line that measures 15 cm? What is the distance on the plan between two points which are 5 m apart?

Ordering and place value

<table>
<tr><td>Number</td><td>

• Take two numbers. Make a number chain by using the rule: *Add the two previous numbers and note the units digit.* What is the shortest chain you can make? The longest?

</td></tr>
<tr><td>Level 4</td><td></td></tr>
</table>

Level 5

• To multiply by 25, multiply by 100 and divide by 4. To multiply by 99, multiply by 100 and subtract one of the number. What is:

      a. 25×28 b. 160×25 c. 17×25
      d. 5×99 e. 16×99 f. 99×11?

Level 5

• An approximate answer for 39×52 is:
      4 tens $\times$ 5 tens $= 20$ hundreds $= 2000$.
What are approximate answers for:

      a. 68×22 b. 31×57 c. 109×42?

Level 5

• This graph shows as percentages the colours of sweet peas growing in a garden. If you picked a bunch of 50, how many of each colour would you expect to get? If there were no pink or purple sweet peas, how many of each of the other colours would you expect to see in a bunch of 100?

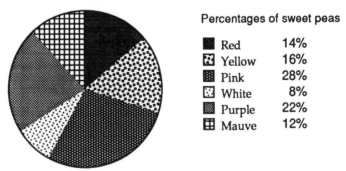

Percentages of sweet peas

■ Red	14%
Yellow	16%
▦ Pink	28%
White	8%
▨ Purple	22%
⊞ Mauve	12%

Level 5

• The answer is 10%. What is the question?

Level 5

• Peter had a bike which cost £100. He sold it to Jo for 10% profit. Jo sold it back to Peter again at a 10% loss. How much did Peter make or lose on the bike? (He made £11.)

Level 5

• What are the values of the missing digits, if $1 \bullet 2 \times 14 \bullet = 24 \bullet 40$? Discuss how to solve this with calculator. (172×145)

Ordering and place value

- The table shows the number of refugees in different countries.

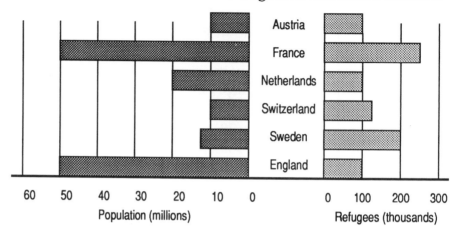

For each country, in every 1000 people, how many would you expect to be refugees?

Imagery

- Put three big boxes on a table and three small cubes. Are there more boxes or more cubes?
  Put a cube in each box. Are there fewer cubes or fewer boxes?
  Put the three cubes into one box. Are there the same number of cubes as boxes?
  Pile the boxes on top of each other. How many boxes are there now? Put the cubes in a tower beside the boxes. Are there more boxes than cubes?
  Hide all three cubes. How many cubes have been hidden?
  Ask the children to imagine three big apples. Would there be fewer apples, or fewer cubes? More apples or more boxes?

- Give every child ten cubes to build something with. Talk about the different shapes. Ask how many cubes in Inderjit's tower, in Samuel's L-shape, in Mandy's box ...

- Imagine a large handful of straws. How many do you think there would be? How could we count them? What about cubes?

- Describe to a small group how to play a counting game.

Ordering and place value

Number	• Imagine choosing two cards from a 1 to 9 pack. If you put them side by side, what is the biggest number you could make? What is the smallest number? What if you chose three cards?
Levels 2, 3	

$$1 \quad 4 \quad 9 \qquad 9 \quad 4 \quad 1$$

Levels 2, 3	• What numbers lie between 23 and 28? Between 123 and 128?
Level 3	• Imagine going to a bank with 252 pence and asking for 10p and £1 coins in exchange. How many of each coin will you get?
Level 3	• My microwave oven has buttons for 10 minutes, 1 minute, 10 seconds and 1 second. How do I get it to show 23 minutes 35 seconds?
Level 3	• Imagine the number four hundred and fifty two. Which digit is on the left? Which is on the right? Change these two digits over. What does your number say now? What is the biggest number you could make with the digits? What is the smallest number you could make?
Levels 2, 3 and 4	• Put these cards with numbers on in order. Now close your eyes while I change two around. Open your eyes. Which did I move?
Levels 3, 4	• Everyone take a calculator. Put one hundred and three in your display. Show your partner. Are your displays the same? Now clear the display and put in two hundred and seventy. Now try six thousand and ninety three. Each time compare with your friends. Try ten thousand and seven, one million and fifteen thousand …
Level 4	• Imagine the number fifty eight thousand, six hundred and fourteen drawn on the blackboard. What is the middle digit? Which digit is in between the six and the three? What does the number say when you read it backwards? What is the largest number you could make using each digit once only?

Ordering and place value

Number

Level 4

Level 4

Level 4

Level 4

Level 4

- The mileometer on a car shows 02699 miles. What will it show when it has gone one more mile? One hundred more miles?

- What numbers do you know that lie between 17 and 18, between 1.7 and 1.8, between 0.17 and 0.18 ...?

- What does *exactly* really mean in these contexts? What does it not mean?

    I am exactly ten years old.
    The temperature today is exactly 10°C.
    I took exactly ten minutes to have a shower.
    My sunflower grew exactly 10 cm last week.

- Research and report on some of the different ways that numbers are used as labels. For example, labelling of pegs, lockers or front doors, post codes, ISBNs, trunk roads, long distance telephone codes, buses, the Dewey system for library books ...

- If you had one million pounds to spend, what would you do?
  If you had to move 1 000 000 cubic millimetres of sand, would you use a bucket, a wheelbarrow, a van or a lorry?
  If you had 1 000 000 seconds to do one of these, would you have one week at Disney World, ten days in Spain, a fortnight skiing, a month on a cruise, or a year going round the world?

Level 5

Level 6

- How would you decide how much chlorine to add to the water in the swimming pool to make it a 1% chlorine solution?

- Estimate the total number of entries in a telephone directory.

Measures

Number	Vocabulary
Level 1	• In PE lessons, can you make *long/short/fast/slow* steps or strides? Make *wide/narrow/thick/thin* shapes.
Level 1	• Tell me about something that is *heavy, light, long, short, thick, thin, wide, narrow, full, empty, hot, cold* … Or is *heavier, lighter, longer … than …*
Levels 1, 2	• When do we use the word *tall*, and when do we use *high*? When do we use *length*, and when do we use *distance*? When do we use *capacity*, and when do we use *volume*?
Levels 1, 2	• What day of the week is it? Which month is your birthday? What took place *today, yesterday, last month, long ago* …? What will take place *soon, tomorrow, next week, next year* …?
Levels 2, 3, 4 and 5	• What units do you know? What are they used to measure?
Levels 3, 4	• On which dates are these festivals this year? For example, *Pancake Tuesday, Ramadan, Maundy Thursday, Hanukkah, Divali, Boxing Day, Thanksgiving, Nawruz, Chinese New Year* …

Level 4	• What is a *decade, decagon, decapod, dean, decimal, dime*? What is the difference between a *decametre* and a *decimetre*? What are *decibels* used to measure?
Level 4	• What is a *centipede, century, centurian*? What is a *cent, centime, centimetre, centigram, centilitre*? What is a *millimetre, millipede, millenium, mile*?

Measures

Number	
Level 5	• What units are used on road signs; in weather forecasts; at a garage, supermarket, chemist's shop, railway station …?
Level 5	• What were or are the following used to measure: *a barley corn; a pole or perch; a chain; a bushel; a fathom*?
Level 5	• What were the origins of *the inch, the foot and the yard*? How are the Irish, the English and the sea mile different?

Mental arithmetic

Level 2	• What questions might have the answer: a width of six straws … a weight of five conkers … a capacity of four cups?
Level 2	• Estimate how many hand spans you can reach, step, jump … What about your friend? How much further can one of you reach, step, jump …?
Level 2	• What is the least number of cubes needed to complete this loop? (5)
Level 2	• Four children each drank half a litre of lemonade. How much did they drink altogether? Jo picked 9kg of apples and May picked 4kg. How many more kilograms of apples did Jo pick? How many times can I cut 4cm from this 9cm ribbon?
Level 2	• It's 10 o'clock now. How many more hours until 3 o'clock? In three days time I am going to the dentist. What day will that be? What date will that be?
Level 3	• How tall are you? How tall are you if you stand on a chair?
Level 3	• The red parcel balances 10 cubes. The blue parcel balances 12 shells. If 3 cubes balance 4 shells, which parcel is heavier?

Measures

Number	• What questions might have the answer: 60 cm ...or 2.5 kg ... or 5 litres ... or 10°C ... or 40 minutes ... or 30 m.p.h?
Levels 3, 4	
Level 4	• Could the coldest day in July be colder than the hottest day in January? If so, how much colder would it be likely to be?
Level 4	• How many cubes are needed to make each of these shapes? How many more cubes would be needed to make each of them into the smallest possible solid cuboid without separating the cubes?

Level 5	• What is your height in feet and inches? What is it in metres? What is the difference in height between the tallest and the shortest person in the class? What capacity is your refrigerator? What about the freezer?
Level 5	• 8 km is about 5 miles. About how many miles is 56 km, 2 km, 1600 km? About how many kilometres is 30 miles, 49 miles?
Level 5	• Estimate the school's floor area. What about its volume?
Level 5	• The scale on a map is 1 to 1000. What is the real length of a line that measures 5 cm on the map? What real distances do you know about the same as this? What is the distance on the map between two points which are 250 m apart?

Imagery

Level 1	• Imagine things you can just manage to carry. Tell me about them. What things would be too heavy to carry? Will this paper be enough to cover this book? How could you tell? Will all these bricks fit into this box? How could you judge?

Measures

Number	
Level 1	• Which do you think takes up more room, this box or this tin? How could we find out?
Level 1	• Which car might roll further than this one? Why do you think so?
Level 2	• Tell me about some things that hold about half a litre. What things hold less than half a litre? What things hold more than half a litre?
Level 2	• Afzhal balanced a ball with 45 shells. Parveen balanced the same ball with 50 shells. Can you explain why?
Levels 2, 3	• Why is it important to have equal (standard) units?
Levels 2, 3	• Here are two different containers. What questions could you ask about them?
Levels 2, 3	• Could an elephant walk through the door of the classroom? What would we need to know about the door? What would we need to know about the elephant?

Level 3	• When will we use the hall for PE, have a spelling test, watch TV, have assembly ...? How long do you think it will take for everyone to get changed, to answer the questions, to sing a hymn ...?

Measures

Number Level 3	• Look at these two leaves. Which has the longer perimeter? Which has the larger area? Why do you think so?

Level 3	• Could a sponge weigh more than a marble?
Level 3	• Can you estimate one minute while I look at the stop watch? Start when I say 'Go'. Tell me when to stop. What events last about one minute? 20 minutes? One hour?
Level 3	• How would you find out the volume of your hand? How would you find out the capacity of your hand?
Levels 3, 4	• How many things can you think of that weigh about 5kg? What things are about 10cm long/tall/wide/deep? What about other measures? What about imperial units?
Level 4	• What things need measuring at home? What is used to measure them? What units are used? What measuring equipment do people carry with them? What measuring equipment do you see in shops? What about other places?
Level 4	• Imagine arranging 16 squares touching edge to edge. Can you make a shape with a perimeter of 18 units? Describe it to me. What about 22 units, 24 units, 26 units, 32 units? What others can you make? Which is the shortest?
Level 5	• Imagine a 'one pint' collection and a 'one gallon' collection. What could be in them?
Level 5	• Which takes up more space – 1kg of potatoes or 1kg of crisps? How should we decide what 'space' means? How could we find out, as accurately as possible, the space taken up by 1kg of potatoes? How could we do this for crisps?

Measures

Number	• How would you set about finding the weight of one paper clip, a single sheet of paper, one grain of rice ...? How would you find the number of grains of rice in 200g?
Level 5	
Level 5	• Estimate, then check with the *Guiness Book of Records*. How tall are the tallest man and the tallest woman? How far can a flea jump? How fast does the cheetah travel?
Level 5	• What would be the best units to use to measure: the length of a river, of the hall, the thickness of a hair; the quantity held by a bath, a bucket, a tablespoon; the weight of a van, a bag of carrots, a packet of crisps, a fly?
Level 6	• This graph tells a story about bath-time. Have a good look at it. Take a few minutes to imagine what happened.

Now take turns to tell each other your stories.

Level 6	• What would a graph look like that showed how hungry you feel during the course of 24 hours?
Level 6	• Does increasing the perimeter ever decrease the area?
Level 6	• What area do you think the leaves of a tree would cover if they were spread all over the ground?
Level 6	• What strategies are useful for estimating measurements?

Doubles and halves

Number	**Vocabulary**
Levels 1, 2	• Use everday situations to use words like *even, odd, double, twice, twin, couple, pair, half, halve, quarter* ...
Level 3	• What is *a double decker, a double bed, a double tooth?* What is *a half-back, a half-holiday, a half-moon, a half-hitch, half-a-dozen, half-a-crown?*

Level 4	• What are or were *doubloons, doublet and hose, double time?* What do *double-barrelled* and *double-breasted* describe? When are the phrases *half-mast* and *half-hearted* used? What do these refer to: *semicircle, semidetached, semiquaver, hemisphere, hemiplegic?* What other phrases about doubles and halves do you know?
Level 4	• What do these words mean: *double, duplicate, quadruple?* What about *dialogue, diameter, diaper, diaphragm, diphthong, diploma?* Or *biscuit, biceps, bigamist, bilingual, biannual, biplane, bivalve, bisect?*
Level 5	• In what units could you measure half a yard, half a mile, half a gallon, half a pound, half a ton, half an acre?

Mental arithmetic

Levels 3, 4	• I have doubled my savings. I started with 20p ... or 75p ... or £1.30 ... or £7.56. How much do I have now? How did you work it out?
Levels 3, 4	• Discuss different ways of finding half of a number such as 74. Now try a different number.

Doubles and halves

<table>
<tr><td>Number</td><td>• I am thinking of a number.
It's half of 16 ... or of 25 ... or of 3.25 ... or of 0.01.
What is it? How did you work it out?</td></tr>
<tr><td>Levels 3, 4 and 5</td><td></td></tr>
</table>

Number

Levels 3, 4 and 5

• I am thinking of a number.
It's half of 16 ... or of 25 ... or of 3.25 ... or of 0.01.
What is it? How did you work it out?

Levels 3, 4 and 5

• One person chooses a number. The next person halves it.
Take turns to keep halving. How far can you go?
One person in the group can check with a calculator.
Try starting with a different number.

Levels 3, 4 and 5

• One person chooses a small whole number.
The next person doubles it.
Take turns to keep doubling. How far can you go?
One person in the group can check with a calculator.
Try starting with a different whole number.

Level 6

Or with a fraction like one-third.

Level 4

• *Half a pound of tuppenny rice. Half a pound of treacle.*
If treacle is 50p and rice 70p for 1lb, what would I pay?
Make up some more questions like this for each other.

Levels 4, 5

• Sit in a circle. One person says a number. The person to the left
says the next number in the chain. Follow this rule.
If the number is even, then halve it. If it's odd, add 1.
Try different starting numbers. Investigate what happens.
What is the longest chain you can make?
Make up another rule for when the number is odd.

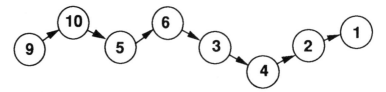

Level 4

• Play *Too big, too small.*
One person thinks of a number between 0 and 100. The others in
the group try to guess what it is. The person who knows the
number may only answer 'too big' or 'too small'.
What is the least number of guesses you need?

Level 5

What if you choose a number between 0 and 1000? How many
guesses do you need now? What is the best strategy?

Doubles and halves

Number
Level 4

- Put the numbers from 1 to 12 in the rings.
  The sum of the numbers in the left-hand ring must be half the
  sum of the numbers in the right-hand ring.
  (The left-hand ring should contain numbers which total 26: for
  example, 2, 5, 8 and 11; or 12, 8 and 6; or 10, 9 and 7; or ...)

Level 4

- My double is 45 more than my half. What number am I? (30)
  Make up some more problems like this.

Level 4

- When you double me and add 2, my two digits are reversed.
  What number am I? (25)

Level 4

- John has as many sisters as brothers, and his sister Julie has half
  as many sisters as brothers. How many children are there? (7)

Levels 4, 5

- How should a burglar balance six bags of loot in two suitcases?
  (29kg + 23kg in one case; the rest in the other)

Levels 4, 5

- There are some goats and ducks around a pond.
  They have 40 heads and 88 feet between them.
  How many goats are there? (4) How many ducks? (36)

Doubles and halves

<table>
<tr><td>

Number

Level 5

</td><td>

- Imagine you have some pieces of dark glass. Each piece reduces by one half the amount of light passing through it. How much is the light reduced after passing through two pieces, five pieces, ten pieces ...?

</td></tr>
<tr><td>

Level 5

</td><td>

- Tara decided to save up. On the first day she saved £1. On the next day she saved £2 and the next day £4. If she kept this up, doubling the amount each day, how much do you think would she have saved after a week? What if she kept it up for a month? Estimate first, then check with a calculator.

</td></tr>
</table>

Imagery

<table>
<tr><td>

Level 1

</td><td>

- In a PE session, can you think of ways of finding half of the number in the class (for example, taking partners, or lining up in two matching lines)? Does everyone have a partner? How many pairs? Find a different partner. How many pairs now? What would happen if two children sat out?

</td></tr>
<tr><td>

Level 2

</td><td>

- Can you point half way along this table. Half way down this chair? Across this book? Along the wall? Can you stand half way to the door? How could you find half this piece of string, or lump of plasticine, or piece of paper? What about quarters?

</td></tr>
<tr><td>

Level 3

</td><td>

- Imagine a square. Fold it in half. What shape is it now? Imagine folding it in half again. What shape is it now?

</td></tr>
<tr><td>

Level 3

</td><td>

- Think of this square. Imagine half of it coloured black and half coloured white. Tell each other what your square looks like. How many different patterns can you think of?

</td></tr>
<tr><td>

Level 3

</td><td>

- A lily in a pond doubles its area every day. It fills the pond completely after 8 days. How many days did it take to fill half the pond? Why?

</td></tr>
<tr><td>

Level 4

</td><td>

- I bought a bottle of lemonade and drank half of it. On each day after that, I drank half of what was left. How long did it take me to finish the lemonade? Why?

</td></tr>
</table>

Doubles and halves

- Imagine a newspaper with 48 pages. What pages are in the centre? (24 and 25)
  When the sheets are taken apart, what pages are printed on the same sheet as page 10? How did you work it out? (9, 39 and 40)
  Make up another problem like this.

- Mrs Khan has a square rose garden with a tree at each corner. How can she double the size of the garden, keeping it square, and keeping the trees in the same position? (Turn the square through 45° and enlarge it)

- Imagine this shape. If it were double the size, what would its area be? (64 square units) Half the size? (4 square units)

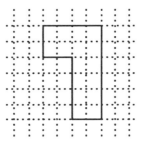

- Imagine folding a long thin strip of paper in half, end to end. Press it flat. There is one fold, and two regions.

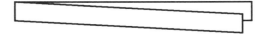

  Imagine folding it in half again. How many folds and regions now?

  What if you halved it six more times? (255 folds, 256 regions)

D

Patterns

Algebra	Vocabulary

Levels 1, 2 and 3	• *Two, four, six, eight … Three, six, nine, twelve …*
	I am going to sing two notes: doh and me. Can you count the number of dohs?
	
	    doh, doh, me, me, doh, doh, me, me, doh, doh, me, me …
	    doh, doh, doh, me, me, doh, doh, doh, me, me …
	
	Now count the number of dohs and mes separately.

Levels 2, 3	• What words do you know that describe patterns? For example, *striped, checked, spotty, polka dot, plaid, scalloped, repeated, random, regular, uniform, half-drop, horizontal, vertical, diagonal, symmetrical, tessellated* … What kinds of patterns do you see on clothes?

Levels 3, 4	• What do these words mean:
	    unit, unifom, union …
	    double, dual, biscuit, bicycle, binoculars …
	    treble, triplet, trivet, triangle, tricycle, trio, tricolour, trinity …
	    quadruple, quadrangle, squadron, quadruped, quadrille, quartet, tetrahedron, tetrarch …
	    pentacle, pentagon, pentathlon, punch, quinquereme, quintet …
	    hexagon, sextant, sextet, siesta, semester, sixpence …
	    heptagon, September …
	    octagon, octopus, octet, octahedron, octogenarian, October …
	    nonagon, noon, November …
	    decagon, decade, decimal, December …?

Level 5	• What words do you know that tell you something special about a number? For example, *odd, even, factor, multiple, divisor, prime, square, cube, power, square root, cube root, triangular* … Can you give some examples of each one?
Level 5	• Sometimes we find the *lowest common multiple* of two numbers by multiplying them together; sometimes we don't. Is there a rule? Is there a rule for finding the *highest common factor*?
Level 6	• In what way are these people associated with numbers: *Fibonacci, Pascal, Napier, Eratosthenes, Pythagoras* …?

Patterns

Algebra	**Mental arithmetic**
Level 2	• Can you describe this pattern? What would happen next? How many blobs? How many sticks?

Levels 2, 3	• Joanne bought a soft drink from the machine. It cost 20p. The machine takes 1p, 2p, 5p and 10p coins in any combination. How did she pay for the drink? What possibilities are there?
Levels 2, 3	• The milkman left 18 bottles of milk at the houses in Baker Street. Some houses had five bottles and all the rest had two bottles each. How many houses are there in Baker Street? (6)
Levels 3	• Estimate the number of shoelace holes in the class.
Level 3	• Suggest ways of making 50p using 5p, 10p and 20p coins. How many different ways can you find?
Level 3	• My pack of 10 stamps contains only 2p and 5p stamps. Discuss the possible values of the pack. (23p, 26p, 29p, 32p, 35p, 38p, 41p, 44p, 47p)
Levels 3, 4	• What numbers could ■ and ▲ stand for if ■ + ▲ = 17? Is there a pattern? What if you use negative numbers?
Levels 3, 4	• Can 15 be made as the sum of consecutive numbers? What about 39? Can you do it in more than one way? What other numbers between 1 and 40 are sums of consecutive numbers?
Levels 3, 4	• I paid £1 exactly for some pencils. What might one pencil have cost, and how many did I get?
Level 4	• Tracey counted her books in fours. She had three left over. When she counted in fives, she had four left over. How many books does she have? (19, or 39, 59, 79 ...) Make up some more problems like this.

95

Patterns

Algebra

Level 4

- Can you make 10 using any three identical digits? For example, $11 - 1 = 10$, or $9 + 9/9 = 10$.
  Now make 20, 30, 40, 50, 60, 70, 80 and 90 using any three identical digits. Can you find different ways of doing it?

Level 4

- I have two 35p stamps and two 20p stamps. What parcels could I send without buying more stamps?
  How many different possibilities are there?
  How do you know you have counted them all?

Level 4

- Can you describe these sequences? Imagine the next few patterns. What would the tenth number in each sequence be?

(1) (2) (3)

(1) (2) (3)

(1) (2) (3)

Level 4

- *On the twelfth day of Christmas, my true love sent to me ...*
  How many things altogether? Did you use any patterns to help?

Level 4

- Take a two-digit number. Reverse it. Find the difference between the number and its reverse. Try some other two-digit numbers and do the same. What do you notice?

Patterns

Algebra	• The number 18 is twice the sum of its digits.
Level 4	
	$$18 = 2 \times (1 + 8)$$
	What numbers are three times, four times, five times, six times, seven times, eight times or nine times the sum of their digits? What do these numbers all have in common?
Level 4	• Use the digits 1, 2 and 3. How many different numbers can you make that are divisible by 2? How many that are divisible by 3? By 4? Can you make a number that is divisible by 5? Why not? What if you used the digits 1, 2, 3 and 4?
Level 4	• If a zero is put between the two digits of a multiple of nine, the new number is also a multiple of nine. What is the number?
Level 4	• Choose a number less than 100. Count round the class. Follow the rule: *If it's even, divide by 2. If it's odd, multiply by 3 and add 1.*
	For example: 17 52 26 13 40 20 10 5 16 8 4 2 1
	Choose another number. What happens this time? What is the longest chain you can make?
Level 5	• The number 4 has exactly three factors: 1, 2 and 4. What other numbers up to 100 have exactly three factors? (Square numbers) What number less than 100 has the most factors? (72 or 96)
Level 5	• What similarities are there between 9 and 49? For example, they both end in 9, both are odd, both less than 50, both square, both squares of odd numbers, both squares of odd primes … Now try two more numbers.
Level 5	• What numbers could ■ and ▲ stand for if $2 \times ■ + ▲ = 20$? Is there a pattern? What if you included decimals? What if you included negative numbers?
Level 5	• A two-digit prime number is still prime when the digits change places. What could the number be? (13, 17, 19, 37 or 79)

Patterns

Algebra

Level 5

- Each number in these four sequences is the sum of the two previous numbers. Can you find the missing numbers?

  a.   1 ☐ 4 ☐ ☐ ☐ ☐ ☐ …

  b.   ☐ ☐ ☐ ☐ ☐ 52 84 ☐ …

  c.   3 ☐ ☐ 7 ☐ ☐ ☐ 50 …

  d.   ☐ ☐ ☐ ☐ ☐ ☐ 12 18 …

Imagery

Level 1

- Close your eyes. Imagine a pattern made from five counters. Open your eyes and describe your pattern to your partner.

Level 1

- Do you have a favourite pattern? Can you describe it to me?

Level 1

- Say a pattern of sounds: for example,

    tick, tick, tock, tick, tick, tock, tick, tick …

  Stop the pattern suddenly. Can you continue it? Try with musical instruments, or in PE with hop, jump, skip.

Levels 1, 2

- Can you make different patterns using the same materials: for example, playing cards?

    red, red, black, red, red, black …
    odd, even, odd, even …
    hearts, clubs, clubs, spades, hearts, clubs, clubs, spades …

  Can you describe it? Can you continue it?
  Change two cards around while the children shut their eyes.
  Can they identify which cards have been changed?

Levels 1, 2

- Can you make and describe the same pattern using different materials?

  ● ● ○ ● ● ○ ● ● ○

  clap clap hop clap clap hop clap clap hop

  3   3   7   3   3   7   3   3   7

Patterns

Algebra Levels 1, 2	• Make a pattern of counters or cubes or beads in different colours and sizes. Can you describe it? Can you continue it? Secretly, take one or two pieces out of the pattern and close up the spaces. Which pieces are missing?
Level 2	• Where can you see patterns of numbers? For example, on coat pegs, on a clock face, on a number line, on graphs …
Level 3	• Play this game using straws and a dice with a friend. Take six turns each to roll the dice and pick up the number of straws shown. Build triangles with your straws. How many straws did you use to make triangles? How many triangles did you make? Adapt the game to make squares or hexagons.
Level 3	• Describe some different patterns you could make using tiles like these in a strip eight tiles long. What about a 2 × 2 square?

Level 3	• Play this game several times. Take turns to put your mark in any one, two or three of 15 squares. The winner is the player who makes an odd number of marks. What is the best strategy?

Level 3	• Imagine some rabbits and some hutches. If one rabbit goes in each hutch, one rabbit is left out. If two rabbits go in each hutch, one hutch stays empty. How many rabbits are there? (4) How many hutches? (3)
Level 4	• Imagine some black dots arranged in seven columns. Starting in the top left corner, and moving from left to right, colour each third dot red. Describe the pattern of the red dots. What would be the pattern if there were six columns? What if there were eight columns?

Patterns

Algebra

Level 4

- Imagine some counters laid out in a row: three red, two blue, three red, two blue and so on.

  What colour is the 4th counter? (Blue)   The 21st counter? (Red)
  In what position is the 6th blue counter?   (15th)
  If there are 46 counters, how many would be red? (28)
  Ask some more questions like these about the counters.

Level 4

- Describe how to complete these patterns.

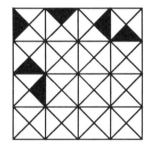

Level 4

- Imagine a large white square. Inside it put a small black circle.
  Make your circle grow so that it just touches each side of your
  square. Inside your circle place another white square. Make
  each of the corners of the square touch the circumference of the
  circle. Inside your square place another black circle. Imagine
  how the pattern might continue. What happens eventually?

Level 5

- In a sequence of 26 hexagons, each hexagon stands for a letter.

   is A. What do you think B might be?

  What do you think has been said in this coded message?

  (MATHS IS GOOD FUN)

100

Shapes

Shape and space	**Vocabulary**
Levels 1, 2 and 3	• Where could you see a *dome, spire, cone, pyramid, sphere, cube, cylinder, prism* ...? What about *circles, triangles, rectangles* ...?

Levels 1 to 4	• What words do you know that help to describe lines? For example, *straight, wavy, rippled, rays, curved, broad, narrow, zig-zag, dotted, dashed, cross-hatched, spiral, intersecting, horizontal, vertical, diagonal, parallel, perpendicular, converging, diverging* ... Can you see any of these in the classroom? Do you know any places outside where you can see them?
Levels 3, 4	• What shapes with curved edges do you know? For example, *circle, semicircle, quadrant, crescent, ellipse* ... Shapes with curved faces? For example, *sphere, cone, cylinder, ovoid, torus* ...
Level 4	• What is a *square dance, square leg, square rig, square cap, square knot, square root* ...?
Level 4	• Look around the classroom. Can you see any *right angles*? What about *acute, obtuse* or *reflex angles*?
Levels 4, 5	• Think about a cube. How many *faces* does it have? How many *edges*? How many *vertices*? How many faces, edges and vertices do other shapes have? Can you spot a pattern?
Level 5	• Can you define a *circle* and these parts of a circle: *circumference, centre, radius, diameter, chord, arc, sector, segment, tangent* ...?

Shapes

	Imagery
Level 1	• Stand opposite a partner. Move your arms, legs, head, and so on. Can your partner reflect your movements? If you move your left arm, which arm does your partner move? What if you stand side by side, and imagine a mirror placed between you?
Levels 1, 2	• What shape is inside this 'feely' bag? How do you know?
Levels 1, 2	• Shut your eyes. Listen while I describe a shape to you … Now open your eyes. Can you pick up the shape I was describing? Now can you describe one for someone else to guess?
Level 2	• Where can you see patterns of shapes around the school? For example, on clothes, in a brick wall, in paving, on a fence, in wall tiles … Can you describe the different patterns?
Levels 2, 3	• You have two 2 × 1 black tiles and two 2 × 1 white tiles. Discuss different ways of tiling a 2 × 2 square grid.
Level 3	• Are these all pentagons? (Yes) Are these all hexagons? (No)

• Make different statements about the properties of this shape.

Level 3

• Imagine a straight line in the air in front of you.
Now, bend your line to make an angle.
Can you bend the line again and make a triangle?
Imagine another straight line.
How many times would you need to bend it to make a square?

Shapes

Shape and space

Level 3

- Describe ways of putting these three shapes together to make a symmetrical shape.

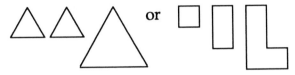

Level 3

- This is half a shape. Describe the different whole shapes you could make. What if it were one quarter of a whole shape? Make up some more problems like this.

Levels 3, 4

- Describe some road signs that are symmetrical.

Levels 3, 4

- Imagine you have some sticks in two different lengths. Imagine making a triangle from three of the sticks. Describe your triangle. Now make a different triangle. How many different triangles can you make? (4)
  What if you had sticks in three lengths? (10)

Levels 3, 4

- Here is a picture of Monty. Without showing the picture, tell your partner how to make him.

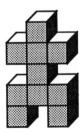

  If you made the smallest doorway to fit round Monty, how many cubes wide would it be? How many cubes tall? How many cubes would you need altogether for the doorway?
  If you made the smallest sentry box for Monty, how many cubes do you think you would you need?
  If you made the smallest packing case with a lid for Monty, how many cubes do you think you would need?
  Make different shapes with cubes, and ask similar questions.

Shapes

Shape and space

Levels 3, 4

• What other ways are there of arranging three circles?

 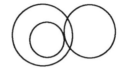

Levels 3, 4

• Imagine a triangle. Call the corners A, B and C.
Which corner is the highest? Which is the furthest right?
Which is the shortest side of your triangle?
Which is the smallest angle?

Levels 3, 4

• Imagine a large white equilateral triangle in front of you.
Now place three small black equilateral triangles inside your
large white triangle. Push one of the small black triangles right
into the corner of the white triangle. Then push the other two
into the other two corners. What shape is the white piece that's
left in the middle?

Level 4

• What shape do you think this envelope would make if it were
opened out and pressed flat?

Level 4

• Imagine a paper square. Imagine folding it in half to make a
rectangle. Now fold it in half to make a small square. Press the
second fold down hard and imagine cutting along it. What
shape will the paper be when you open it up? What if you start
with another square but fold across the diagonal?

Level 4

• How many angles less than 360° are there altogether in this
diagram? (12)

What if there were five lines? (20)

104

Shapes

Shape and space

Levels 4, 5

- Imagine a clock with two hands. What angle does the hour hand turn through in 2 hours, 10 hours, 15 hours, 20 minutes? (30° for each hour; 10° for 20 minutes)
  What angle does the minute hand turn through in 10 minutes, 20 minutes, one hour? (30° for each five minutes)

Levels 4, 5

- Imagine the long hand of a clock pointing to the two. The little hand is between the three and the four. What time is it? (3.10)
  Suppose the time is ten o'clock and that you see the clock in a mirror. What time do the hands seem to say? (2.00)
  Imagine that you see the clock in a mirror and the hands of the clock seem to say quarter past six. What time is it really? (5.45)
  When are the clock face and its image the same? (12.00, 6.00)

Level 5

- Imagine a square. Cut a small piece off each corner. What shape is it now? How do you know? What if you made bigger cuts? What if you started with a triangle, a pentagon ...?

Level 5

- Can you describe these patterns? In what ways are they the same? In what ways are they different?

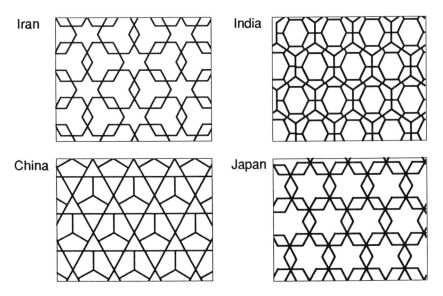

Shapes

Shape and space Level 5	• Imagine a wooden cube. One edge has a red bead at each end. How many edges have a red bead at one end? (4) How many edges have no bead at either end? (7) What if the two red beads were at the two diagonally opposite corners of one face? (One bead 6; no bead 6) What if they were at the opposite ends of a diagonal through the centre of the cube? (One bead 6; no bead 6)
Level 5	• Imagine a solid wooden cube painted red. Imagine cutting off one corner. What is the shape of the cut surface? (A triangle)
Level 5	• Imagine a rectangle drawn in the air in front of you. Label the corners A, B, C and D. Now tilt your rectangle so that C is directly above A. Where are the other two corners? Is the line BD horizontal?
Levels 5, 6	• Imagine a cube standing on a face with a red bead at each vertex. The red beads lie in two horizontal layers (planes), with four beads in each layer. Tilt the cube on to one edge so it balances. How many horizontal layers of red beads are there now? (3) How many beads are there in each layer? (2, 4, 2) Tilt the cube again until it balances on one vertex. How many horizontal layers of red beads? (4) How many beads in each layer? (1, 3, 3, 1)
Levels 5, 6	• Imagine a right-angled triangle. Rotate it about its shortest side. What shape is formed? Now imagine it rotated about its longest side (the hypotenuse). What shape is formed now?

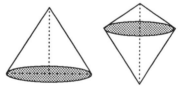

Imagine a circle. What shape do you get if you rotate it about a diameter? (A sphere) What if you rotate it about a line outside the circle? (A torus – a doughnut shape)

Imagine a square. Rotate it about one side. What shape is formed? (A cylinder) What if you rotate it about a diagonal? (Two identical cones joined by their bases)

Shapes

- Look at some traditional Chinese paintings made up of just a few lines. Discuss the lines, their length, thickness, curvature or closeness, or the angle which one makes with another.

To draw bamboo: Avoid making stems like drumsticks. Avoid making joints of equal length. Avoid lining up the bamboos like a fence. Avoid placing the leaves to one side. Avoid criss-crossing like a net. When you put brush to paper, work boldly. Do not hesitate. Mai-mai Sze.

In China, bamboo grows in thick groves, sometimes to a height of 30 metres. Close your eyes and imagine painting a bamboo plant in the Chinese style, following Mai-mai Sze's advice. Consider the lines you will draw first and the thickness of your brush. Practise the movement of your hand through the air. Now try, using white paper and black paint.

Level 6

- The artist Claude Monet said:

When you go out to paint, try to forget what objects you have before you, a tree, a house, a field, or whatever. Merely think that here is a little square of blue, here an oblong of pink, here a streak of yellow, and paint it just as it looks to you, the exact colour and shape.

In small groups, look at some postcards of Monet's paintings. Can you decide what shapes Monet saw before he began to paint? Look at some views around the school, either from the windows or outside, or at some photographs of different scenes. What shapes do you see?

Position and direction

Shape and space	**Vocabulary**
Level 1	• Can you sit or stand or lie: *next to/behind/in front of/beside/at the side of* … your partner? Who is sitting behind Manuel? Give instructions to move making use of words like *up, down, left, right, forwards, backwards, towards, away from, over, under, through, across, along, clockwise, anticlockwise* …
Level 1	• Look round the classroom. What is *higher than, lower than, above, below, between, in the middle of, at the edge of, in the corner of* …?
Level 1	• Using a magnetic board and transport shapes, can you: put the red aeroplane *above* the boat; put the van *below* the green aeroplane; put the car *beside* the van?

Imagery

Level 1

• This diagram shows eight children with coloured hats standing in a circle. They are facing inwards.

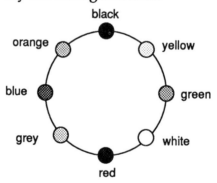

Which hat is to the left of the blue one? To the right of the black one? To the left of the green one? To the right of the grey one? What if they are facing outwards? Make up your own questions.

Levels 2, 3

• Can you describe to each other the directions to take to walk from the school to the Town Hall?

Levels 2, 3

• Is it further from the school to the mosque, from the school to the station, or the school to the High Street? Why do you think so?

Position and direction

Shape and space Levels 2, 3	• Imagine the numbers 1, 2, 3 and 4 placed in a line so that no two consecutive numbers are next to each other. What number would you make? What if you used 1, 2, 3, 4 and 5?
Level 3	• Without turning the paper, can you describe two different routes from Calcot to Birch End?

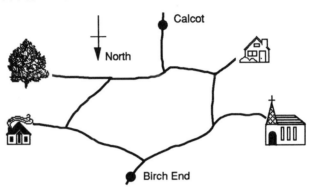

Level 3	• Talk about things that turn: for example, the hands of a clock, taps, see-saws, doors, lids of jars, pages of a book, the sails of a windmill, a helicopter rotor, swings, scissors, steering wheels ... Which turn about a point and which about a line?
Level 3	• What happens to shadows during the course of a sunny day?
Level 3	• Play Noughts and Crosses with a difference. Take turns to tell the other player where to put a mark.

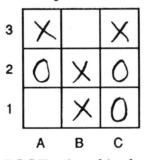

Level 3	• Imagine the word BOOT printed in the air in front of you. Imagine the word SALE printed directly beneath it. Which letter is directly above the A? Which is below the T? Which letter is diagonally to the right of the S? Change over the third letter of the top word with the second letter of the bottom word. What do the words say now?

Position and direction

Shape and space

Level 3

- Describe a path from the lake, around the house to the tree. Now make up some more routes.

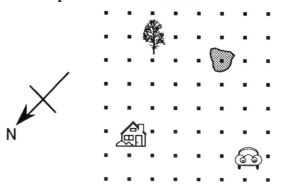

Level 3

- Imagine a cube placed on the top left square of a 3 × 3 board. Describe a route to move the cube from its starting point to the bottom right square. The cube may only move horizontally to the right or vertically downwards. Now describe another route. How many different routes are there altogether? (6)

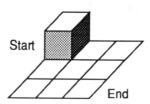

Level 4

- The first rhombus has a black spot in it. Without turning your head, and without turning the paper, decide where the black spot would go in the other three. Explain why.

Level 4

- Mark a 6 × 6 grid and label the lines with coordinates. Take turns to tell the other player where to put a counter. The winner is the first to see four of their own counters at the corners of a square.

Level 4

- A cyclist arrived at a point where three roads met, but the sign-post had fallen down. How can he work out which road to take? Discuss in small groups. (Replace the sign-post so that the correct arm points to where he has come from)

Position and direction

Shape and space Level 4	• It is possible to draw capital letters like M or L with a single stroke. Others, like T or G, need more than one stroke. Which of these letters can be drawn with a single stroke: H O U S E? Which letters of your name can be drawn with a single stroke?
Level 4	• Imagine a game of Noughts and Crosses. Nought starts and goes in the bottom left square. Cross goes in the bottom right square. Nought goes in the middle square. Cross now goes in the top right square. Where should Nought go now? Play an imaginary game of Noughts and Crosses with a partner.
Level 4	• Take two identical copies of a road map and work in pairs. One person chooses where to start and tells the other. The first person now gives directions for getting from the chosen place to another unnamed place. Can the other person trace the route?
Level 5	• These are three positions of the same cube. What letter is opposite L? (H)
Level 5	• Take an Ordnance Survey map. Choose a vantage point. Discuss the features that you think can be seen when looking in a particular direction. Can you sketch them?
Level 5	• You will need black paint, a fine brush and some 10 cm × 10 cm squares of paper marked like this. Choose one of these Chinese characters, without telling your partner. Give instructions so that he or she can reproduce the character. It helps if you work from the top to the bottom. 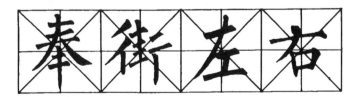

Collecting and presenting data

Handling data	Vocabulary
Levels 1 to 4	• If you have a set of numbers, what might be useful to know about them? For example, how many numbers in the set, the biggest and smallest numbers, the range of the numbers, the most common number, the average number, the middle number, how they look when arranged in order …
Levels 3, 4	• Find out as much as you can about counting devices and tell each other about them. For example, a counting frame, a tally stick, the Incan *quipu* …

Level 4	• Compare the everyday meaning of words with mathematical meanings: for example, *set, table, list, average, mean, range.*
Level 4	• What does *average* mean? In what circumstances is it used?
Levels 4, 5	• What is information? For example, *news, facts, instructions, messages, notices, bulletins, reports, data* … What does it look like? For example, *words, pictures, numbers, signs, symbols, codes, sounds, smells, tastes* …
Levels 4, 5	• What can you do with data? For example, it can be searched and a selection made. It can be counted, arranged in order or classified in groups. It can be presented in a *list, table, diagram, chart, graph, sketch, model, map, plan, flow chart* …
Levels 4, 5 and 6	• Samuel Johnson said: *Knowledge is of two kinds. We know a subject ourselves, or we know where we can find information upon it.* Where can you find information? For example, in a museum or library or archive, on a sign-post … In a dictionary, atlas, street map, encyclopaedia, cookery book, … In a register, newspaper, church record, telephone directory, catalogue, timetable, calendar, bank statement, the *Radio Times* … In a photograph album, on audio tape, video film, on microfiche, in a computer database, on teletext pages, on video disc … Where else?

Collecting and presenting data

Mental arithmetic

- How many children have some crisps in their lunch box? How many have fruit? Who has some chocolate? Who has a bread roll? Do more children have crisps than have fruit? How many more? Do fewer children have a bread roll than have chocolate? What is the difference between the number with a roll and the number with fruit?

Level 2

- These birds visited a bird table when we watched for 5 minutes.

Blackbird	🐦 🐦 🐦 🐦	4
Blue tit	🐦 🐦	2
Thrush	🐦	1
Sparrow	🐦 🐦 🐦 🐦 🐦	5

Which kind of bird came twice? How many more sparrows than blue tits came? How many birds came altogether? Which birds didn't come? Which bird came most often? Can you think why?

Level 3

- The 13th June is a Wednesday. What day of the week is 29th June? What about 4th June? What date is the first Sunday in June, the last Saturday, the third Thursday ...?

Level 4

- What is the fastest train between Birmingham New Street and Reading? Between Coventry and Oxford? Oxford and Reading?

Birmingham New Street	0941	1006	1106	1236
Birmingham International	0950	1017	1116	1247
Coventry	1012	1031	1129	1301
Leamington Spa	1026	....	1143	1315
Banbury	1046	....	1203	....
Oxford	1107	1121	1224	1354
Reading	1131	1156	1250	1425

Collecting and presenting data

- A scientist testing the quality of a sample of peas counted the number in each pod.

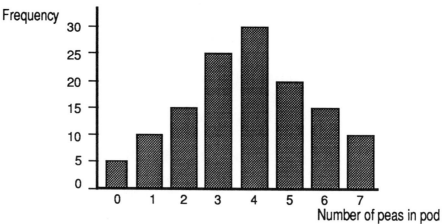

What was the most common number of peas in a pod? (4)
How many pods contained just two peas? (15)
How many pods were tested? (130) How many peas? (495)
What was the average (mean) number of peas in a pod? (3.8)

Imagery

- If we made a set of things that are red, what could be in it?
  What if we made a set of things that are not red? What about
  sets made of wood/not made of wood, flexible/not flexible?

- Play *Stand up, Sit down*.
  Stand up all the children who are wearing navy socks.
  Why isn't Ali in the set? Why isn't Ben in the set?
  What can we call the set of children standing up?
  What can we call the set of children sitting down?
  Now try with:
      all those who are wearing something green;
      all those who are not six years old;
      all those with blue eyes **and** with a younger sister;
      all those wearing earrings **and** not wearing black shoes;
      all those who came to school on a bus **or** in a car.

- How could we sort pieces of fabric, shapes, pebbles, letters of
  the alphabet, coins, flowers, cheeses, greetings cards ...?

Collecting and presenting data

Handling data

Level 2

- Put out these playing cards on a table top so children can see them, then shuffle them. Secretly remove one, then ask children to guess what it is.

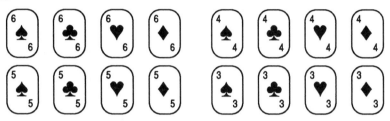

Levels 2, 3 and 4

- Play *Aunt Agatha*. As pupils spot patterns, they can offer clues.

  Aunt Agatha likes   eggs   but not   bacon

                          butter   but not   bread

                          carrots   but not   potatoes

  (In this example, she likes food with double letters)

Level 3

- Mary was given a box of bricks for her birthday. The graph shows how many bricks of each colour were in the box. Use the graph to make up a box of bricks the same as Mary's.

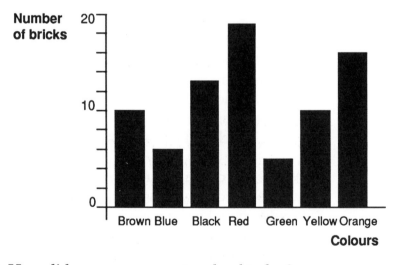

Level 3

- How did everyone come to school today?

  What was the most common way?

  How should we present the information?

  How would the information change if no buses were running?

  How would it change if the weather were different?

  How would it change if there were twice as many children?

Collecting and presenting data

- What can you tell from comparing these two graphs? What do you think the reasons for the differences are?

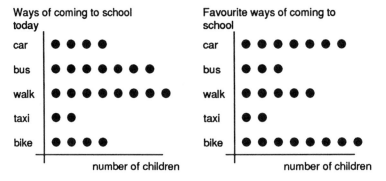

Level 3

- Sort a set of dominoes according to their total number of spots. Arrange each group in a tower. Put the towers in order: for example, no spots, one spot, two spots ... twelve spots. What shape does your 'graph' make? Is it symmetrical? Why? Which is the most common total of spots? (Six spots)

Levels 3, 4

- How could you collect information about:

  coats or jackets worn to school;
  how much shelf space is needed for lunch boxes;
  which food birds prefer;
  how a plant grows over time;
  which school lunches are the most popular;
  TV programmes between 6pm and 9pm;
  which packet of cereal gives best value for money?

  Would you design a questionnaire or ask people? If so, what questions would you need to ask? Who would you ask? Would you take any measurements? If so, of what? Would you look things up? If so, what and where? Would you go to the library? Would you make any phone calls?

Levels 3, 4

- Plan a party. What information will you need? For example, who to invite, what to eat and drink (recipes, quantities, prices), where to hold it (arrangements of tables and chairs), songs to sing and games to play (looking up songs and games, planning how long each will take).

Collecting and presenting data

Handling data

Levels 3, 4

- What information would you need to organise a seating plan for the school play, a second-hand book sale, a visit to London ...?

Levels 3, 4 and 5

- What information would you collect, where would you get it from, and what would you do with it, in order to find out:

   if red is the most popular colour in the class;
   whether more babies are born in the spring or in other seasons;
   which was the hottest day last year;
   whether children watch television more than adults;
   where to position the computer in the classroom;
   if it is safe to cross the road;
   whether or not to buy a pair of shoes;
   what to choose from the menu for a school lunch;
   how to find a particular book in the library;
   how quickly everyone could get out if there were a fire;
   what life was like 50 years ago;
   whether the school fête was more successful this year;
   which balls bounce highest;
   how fashion trends differ for 11-year-old girls and boys;
   what jobs are available to teenagers?

   Would you use a computer to help you? If so, how?

Levels 5, 6

- When would you use a sample in your survey and when would you use a census (count) of all the population involved? When you use a sample, how do you decide on the sample to be sure that it is fair? For example, who would you ask to find out which was the most popular brand of crisps? How many would you ask? How would you choose them? How old would they be? Where would they live? How much money would they be likely to have?

Collecting and presenting data

Handling data Levels 5, 6	• How might these survey samples be biased: a survey on favourite sports carried out with 10-year-old boys; a survey of traffic passing the school gate between 8 and 9 am; a survey in the High Street on voting in a general election?
Level 6	• For what purposes do we require information? What is the difference between fact and opinion? Collect and discuss some newspaper graphs or charts that show facts or opinions.
Level 6	• Look at a range of claims from advertisers or media presenters. Are they likely to be true or false? Are they misleading? Why? For example: prices slashed; eight out of ten cats prefer Bouncers; this is our biggest ever offer; only one soap powder washes whiter than white; an area of rain forest the size of Wales is cut down each year; the rate of inflation is falling.
Level 6	• What questions about schools would each of the following groups be interested in: pupils, parents, teachers, governors, politicians, the general public?
Level 6	• What questions are best avoided in surveys because of their potential sensitivity to people as individuals?
Level 6	• Comment on these results of two maths tests. The second test was taken two weeks after the first. Marks were out of 20.

	Marks in Test 1	Marks in Test 2
Paul	7	8
Amrit	11	14
Fay	10	13
Sabina	9	10
Peter	8	10
Average mark	8	11
No. below average	2	3

Probability

Handling data	**Vocabulary**
Level 2	• Discuss *chance* and *likelihood*, what is likely to happen *always, sometimes, never*, what is *possible, impossible, certain, uncertain, lucky, unlucky* ...
Level 3	• What is associated with a four-leaved clover, horseshoe, black cat, touching wood, picking up a pin, walking under a ladder, breaking a mirror, opening an umbrella indoors? Is it justified?

Level 3	• How many everyday phrases do you know connected with luck and what do they mean? For example, *good luck, better luck next time, worse luck, beginner's luck, out of luck, try one's luck, luck of the draw* ... Or *take a chance, an even chance, half a chance, stand a chance, the main chance* ...? Or *it's not fair, fair and square, fair weather, fairground* ...?
Level 4	• What are *odds* of two to one? What are *long odds*? What do these phrases mean: *what's the odds, it makes no odds, being at odds with*?
Level 4	• Give some examples of things that are *fair, biased, random* ...
Level 5	• Discuss these quotations.

Benjamin Franklin:
Nothing can be said to be certain, except death and taxes.
Samuel Lover:
There's luck in odd numbers.
Duke of Wellington:
Possible? Is anything impossible? Read the newspapers.

Probability

Handling data	Mental arithmetic
Level 3	• Five goals were scored in a football match. How many different final scores could there be? (6)
Level 3	• This dice has two red faces, two blue faces and two yellow faces. If I roll the dice, how many different results are possible? (3)
Level 4	• What is the chance of getting an odd score on a 1 to 6 dice? (1/2) A score less than five? (2/3) A score that is either even or less than five? (5/6)
Level 4	• If you toss a dice 30 times, about how many times would you expect to get 1? (About 5) Why? What if you tossed it 300 times? (About 50)
Level 5	• Imagine picking a playing card from the set of 52 face down on the table. What is the probability that the card is red? (1/2) That it is a red heart? (1/4) That it is the ace, king, queen or jack of hearts? (1/13) That it is the two of hearts? (1/52)
Level 5	• If one domino is picked randomly from the whole set, what is the probability that it is a double? (7/28 or 1/4) That the total number of spots is odd? (12/28 or 3/7) That the total number of spots is seven? (3/28)
Levels 5, 6	• How many ways can you get a total score of six by rolling two dice? (5) What about other total scores? What other questions could you ask about the two dice?
Levels 5, 6	• If you tossed two coins 100 times, about how many times would you expect to get two tails? (About 25) Why?

Probability

Handling data

Levels 5, 6

- In a race for five horses, their odds are 11-8, 2-1, 7-4, 12-7 and 3-2. If you bet £1, on which horse could you win the most? (At 2-1)

Levels 5, 6

- There are 12 red balls in one bag and 12 blue balls in another bag. Six balls are taken from the red bag and put in the blue bag, which is thoroughly shaken up. Six balls are then taken from the mixed bag and put back in the red bag. What is each bag now likely to contain? (8 red and 4 blue, and 4 red and 8 blue)

Imagery

Level 2

- Are some people luckier than others? Why do you think so? Have you a lucky number? Why do you think it's lucky?

Level 2

- What things are certain to happen? What things are impossible and can never happen? What might happen, but might not?

Level 3

- What vehicles are very likely to pass the school gate between 10 and 11 am? Why? What vehicles would definitely not pass by? Why not? What vehicles would be possible but not very likely? Why? Would your ideas be different if your school was in a completely different place? What about a different time of day?

Level 3

- Finish off sentences which begin: *I am less likely to ... if I ...*   For example, *I am less likely to have an accident if I cross the road at a pedestrian crossing*. Then try finishing sentences which begin: *I am more likely to ... if I ...*

Probability

Handling data
Level 3
	• Talk about everyday events, what is likely or unlikely, and what factors might influence or change the likelihood.
	
	    Is it more likely to rain in April or in June?
	    How certain is it that an egg will break if I drop it?
	    What is impossible/unlikely/possible/likely/certain to happen in school this week?
	    How many pupils are likely to take a school lunch next week?

Levels 3, 4 and 5	• What degree of risk (large, moderate, small) is associated with:
	
	    crossing the road;
	    eating peanuts;
	    motor racing;
	    walking through a field of long grass;
	    catching whooping cough;
	    swimming in a river and swimming in a swimming pool?
	
	    In each case, how could the risk be reduced?

Levels 3, 4	• Think of an event, and discuss all the possible outcomes: e.g.
	
	    My birthday this year is on Sunday/Monday/Tuesday ... (7 outcomes)
	    The next person to walk by will be male/female (2 outcomes)
	    If I pick a Smartie it will be red/yellow/brown ... green (8 outcomes)
	
	    Can you think of events which have six possible outcomes?

Level 4	• A baker makes pies in three different sizes with four different fillings. How many different pies are made? (12)

122

Probability

Handling data	• This bag holds lots of red cubes and two white cubes. What do you think will be the colour of the next cube I take out of the bag? Why?
Level 4	
Level 4	• On a line numbered from 0 to 1, where would you place these: possible, probable, highly improbable, certain, uncertain, likely, unlikely, very likely, more than likely, even chance, fifty-fifty, never, always, beyond reasonable doubt, a sure thing ...?

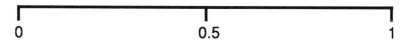

0	0.5	1

Level 4	• Describe the chance of something happening using words: for example, it is unlikely to rain tomorrow. Then describe the same thing using numbers: for example, there is a one in ten chance that it will rain tomorrow. Make up some more examples.

Level 4	• What events might have the probability of 1 in 2? (Tossing a coin for heads or tails, the sex of a new baby, rolling an even number on a dice, a postcard through the door landing picture side up, picking a red card from a pack of cards ...)
Level 4	• Some people say that it is harder to throw a six on a dice. Is this true? How could you test it?

Probability

Handling data	• What might be a fair way of sharing three 1p pieces between two children, assuming that none of the coins can be broken? (Perhaps toss each coin, or give one each and toss the third)
Level 4	
Level 4	• Four pairs of socks are jumbled up in a drawer. If you put your hand in without looking, how many socks must you take out to be certain of getting a matching pair? (5)
Level 4	• Twins can be identical or non-identical. What possibilites are there for triplets? (Three identical; two identical, one not; all non-identical) What about quins? (Seven different possibilites)
Levels 4, 5	• If a carpenter has two different colours of glass to fit these three panes, how many different windows can be made? (8) What if there are three different colours? (27)

Levels 5, 6	• What information would you collect, where would you find it, and what would you do with it, in order to find out:

if the number 73 bus is likely to be late;
if the weather on June 15th is likely to be fine;
if a girl of 14 was likely to be in domestic service in the 19th century?

Levels 5, 6	• Discuss how you would find out the probability of the next car passing the school gate being red.
Level 6	• Two squares are coloured at random on a 3 × 3 grid. What is the probability that they are next to each other? (12/36 or 1/3)

Level 6	• The final score in a match was 2-3. How many different ways could it have been reached? (10) Investigate other final scores.